DRIVING
GROWTH
THROUGH
INNOVATION

Other books by Robert B. Tucker

Winning the Innovation Game

Managing the Future

Win the Value Revolution

DRIVING
GROWTH
THROUGH INNOVATION

How leading firms are transforming their futures

ROBERT B. TUCKER

BK®

BERRETT-KOEHLER PUBLISHERS, INC.
San Francisco

Berrett-Koehler Publishers, Inc.
235 Montgomery Street, Suite 650
San Francisco, CA 94104-2916
Tel: (415) 288-0260   Fax: (415) 362-2512
www.bkconnection.com

ORDERING INFORMATION

Quantity sales. Special discounts are available on quantity purchases by corporations, associations, and others. For details, contact the "Special Sales Department" at the Berrett-Koehler address above.

Individual sales. Berrett-Koehler publications are available through most bookstores. They can also be ordered direct from Berrett-Koehler: Tel: (800) 929-2929; Fax: (802) 864-7626; www.bkconnection.com

Orders for college textbook/course adoption use. Please contact Berrett-Koehler:
Tel: (800) 929-2929; Fax: (802) 864-7626.

Orders by U.S. trade bookstores and wholesalers. Please contact Publishers Group West, 1700 Fourth Street, Berkeley, CA 94710. Tel: (510) 528-1444; Fax (510) 528-3444.

Berrett-Koehler and the BK logo are registered trademarks of Berrett-Koehler Publishers, Inc.

Printed in the United States of America

Berrett-Koehler books are printed on long-lasting acid-free paper. When it is available, we choose paper that has been manufactured by environmentally responsible processes. These may include using trees grown in sustainable forests, incorporating recycled paper, minimizing chlorine in bleaching, or recycling the energy produced at the paper mill.

Library of Congress Cataloging-in-Publication Data
Tucker, Robert B.
   Driving growth through innovation : how leading firms are transforming their futures / by
   Robert B. Tucker.
       p.   cm.
   Includes bibliographical references and index.
   ISBN 1-57675-187-2
   1. Technological innovations—Management.   2. Technological innovations——United
States—Management—Case Studies.   I. Title.
   HD45.T797   2002
   658.4′063—dc21   2002071259

FIRST EDITION
07   06   05   10   9   8   7   6   5   4   3   2

Designed by Detta Penna
Copyedited by Pat Brewer
Proofread by Cathy Baehler
Indexed by Joan Dickey

To Carolyn

Contents

What It Takes
to Drive Growth

How will you drive growth in your company? The solution that this book puts forth is explainable in one word: innovation. Although cost-cutting efforts can build your bottom line because they increase the spread between gross and net, they cannot increase top- line revenue; they cannot fuel growth.

To do that you must offer customers something new. Something that they cannot get anywhere else but from you, something that solves their problem in a superior way. To do that you must come out with products and strategies that cause existing and new customers to buy more of what you sell. To do that you need to go after new customer groups with new offerings that add revenue to your top and your bottom line. Doing these things is the essence of innovation.

There's nothing new about innovation. Companies innovated to get where they are today. And surveys indicate that managers in a broad range of industries are well aware of the importance of innovation as the key driver of growth, profitability, and competitive advantage. A PricewaterhouseCoopers survey of 399 global executives found innovation easily surpassing globalization, industry convergence, and even e-business as their top strategic challenge.

There's only one problem. Despite a *belief* that their ability to innovate has the most potential to help them achieve future growth, other surveys reveal a strong sense of *inadequacy* in improving performance in this arena. An Arthur D. Little survey of 669 global executives finds that "fewer than one in four believe they have fully mastered the art of deriving business value from innovation." Put simply, there is a gap between what managers know they must do to achieve growth, and what they are often able to do in practice.

This book is designed to help you and your company achieve levels of growth uncommon in your industry by approaching innovation in a fundamentally different way.

In most companies today, the practice of innovation can be likened to the mating of pandas: infrequent, clumsy, and often ineffective. Its practice is largely unchanged from 20 years ago. While the world has changed drastically, the practice of innovation remains ad hoc, unsystematic, piecemeal, and "seat of the pants."

Innovation is at the point where the discipline of quality was in 1980. Then, quality was a department. You could isolate it on a company's organization chart. Today quality in most firms has become an embedded *process* that makes it everyone's responsibility. It's ingrained in the culture, in the way they do business.

In most firms today, innovation is still largely confined to specific, select departments, which have a monopoly on new ideas. "You're going to have to explain what you mean by innovation to these people," whispered the CEO of a Fortune 500 food company just as I was about to address his 200 top leaders. "They think of innovation as R&D or marketing or product development."

The right, and indeed the responsibility, to conceive and champion new ideas is still in the hands of a select few. Rank and file employees, or, as we will refer to them in this book, individual contributors, are far removed from the process. The prevailing attitude is: "If we wanted your ideas, we'd have asked for them."

Because no one is in charge of innovation, or of setting stretch goals in this area of the company, the focus is on risk-averse, incremental improvements. For a consumer products company this might mean putting blue flakes in their laundry detergent and calling it "new and improved." Or a software firm adding a new bell or whistle to a new version and calling it a "major upgrade." Or a soft drink maker introducing yet another one-calorie beverage and calling it "revolutionary."

Today's savvy customers have grown tired of such window dressing. They want new solutions that bring real benefits. They want companies to help them solve their problems in superior ways. They want meaningful choices, and better value propositions. Often they are disappointed.

So are the companies and their shareholders. Because much of the innovation taking place today is incremental, so is its impact on growth. Little ventured, little gained. Other firms, after years of incremental innovation, suddenly throw millions or even billions of dollars at ideas that are poorly conceived, poorly timed, and poorly executed, only to have near-catastrophic consequences.

Such approaches are inadequate to achieving growth in the 21st century enterprise.

This book isn't meant to be an academic treatise on innovation or to offer you theories about how innovation should be practiced. Instead, it is a synthesis of options based on what leading companies are doing to rev up growth and earnings rates using innovation as their vehicle. But it doesn't stop there. *Driving Growth Through Innovation* uses their experiences to actively guide you and your company in designing your own innovation strategy such that you achieve levels of growth not only uncommon in your industry, but uncommon in comparison to all other businesses.

The "field" of innovation is recent. So recent, in fact, that books in this subject area have tended to reflect the "siloed" worldview still found in many companies. As such, they focus on a narrow part of the whole field: strategy innovation, say, or new product development, or how to solve problems more creatively. Or even how to set up a company suggestion program to better manage ideas. All of these subtopics are important. Yet approaching them piecemeal will bring piecemeal results.

The premise of this book is that these seemingly disparate issues must be integrated into a single overarching strategy if they are to be mobilized in the quest for growth. That's why this book summarizes and condenses the key issues of innovation; it is written to enable you and your team to actively move through each chapter and develop a blueprint to redesign your firm's innovation process holistically.

Today, inside a small but growing group of companies, progress is being made to innovate the innovation process. To turn innovation into a systematic, embedded process that unfailingly drives revenue momentum. These Innovation Vanguard companies, such as Citigroup, EDS, Medtronic, Colgate-Palmolive, Borg-Warner, and Royal Dutch/Shell, have redesigned every step and stage of how they bring new ideas to life for greater speed, quicker payback, and more consistent revenue momentum.

These companies encourage ideas from everybody and every-where in the organization, not just from traditional new product development departments. Using highly unconventional methods, they seek out the unmet and unarticulated needs of customers. They prototype ideas more quickly and assess feasibility more intelligent-ly. They fund new ventures differently. And they establish "idea management" systems to ensure that high potential ideas are launched into the marketplace faster, with broader involvement than ever before.

Principles for Driving Growth Through Innovation

Examining practices of these Innovation Vanguard companies throughout this book will guide you in designing and implementing your own innovation process. These firms have discovered that, to drive growth through innovation, you must embrace five essential principles into your own unique approach:

Principle 1: Innovation Must Be Approached as a Discipline

To practice innovation as a discipline means first and foremost that you distinguish between creativity (coming up with ideas) and inno-vation (bringing them to top- and bottom-line results for the com-pany).

Companies sometimes seek to promote creativity, by, for exam-ple, sending their people to facilitated brainstorming sessions. In a cover article in *Inc. Magazine* several years ago, a reporter was allowed to participate in one such session at a leading ideation center, and write about the methods used. The article detailed how a team of managers from a mid-sized food company facing flat sales growth was led through various proprietary lateral thinking exercises and came away with 75 high potential ideas. But three years later, we were told that not a single idea became a product that made it into

Principles for Driving Growth Through Innovation

1. Innovation must be approached as a discipline.

2. Innovation must be approached comprehensively.

3. Innovation must include an organized, systematic, and continual search for new opportunities.

4. Innovation must involve everyone in the organization.

5. Innovation must be customer-centered.

the marketplace. Blaming the firm's "corporate structure and management," the spokesperson lamented that "It's hard to get ideas through an organization."

Such sessions are incredibly fun and often produce lots of new possibilities and plenty of excitement. But nothing happens because innovation, or inventing the future as it's sometimes called, is not a *discipline,* and ideas, no matter how good, get pummeled by the pressures of the present.

Often, companies will claim they have "too many creative ideas" rather than too few. But this too is symptomatic—no comprehensive "idea to implementation" method is in place to separate the winners from the duds.

Innovation-adept firms know that disciplined innovation is not an oxymoron, but a necessary rigor that results, ultimately, in a higher batting average of hits—ideas that bring greater value to customers, and thereby, greater value to the bottom line.

Innovation-adept firms know that the only thing that separates them from competitors is the skills, knowledge, commitment, and *innovation* abilities of their people. Teaching innovation as a discipline involves showing people how to think through their ideas and to know which ones are in alignment with the goals of the business. Teaching the discipline of innovation involves showing people how to champion and sell their ideas, how to find resources, and how to overcome obstacles and build coalitions of support.

Like all disciplines, people get better with practice. Like other disciplines, those who practice it evolve and share a common language. They never stop making mistakes because mistakes are an inevitable part of the process. They simply make less obvious mistakes. They instruct each other and hone collective and individual skills through learning and practice.

Principle 2: Innovation Must Be Approached Comprehensively

Innovation can't be confined to one department or an elite group of star performers. It cannot be assigned to a skunkworks far afield from the main organization and insulated from the company's bureaucracy. It must permeate the company, and it must encompass new products, services, processes, strategies, business models, distribution channels, and markets. It must become part of the DNA of the entire organization.

A comprehensive approach to innovation means that it becomes the responsibility and way of operating of business units and functional departments, whether purchasing, operations, finance, or human resources, just as much as it is for new product development or marketing.

What motivates managers and leaders across the organization to embrace innovation broadly and give it ongoing priority? Metrics. Innovation Vanguard firms have discovered that the adage "that which gets measured gets done" is no less true of the innovation process than any other. While the most common yardstick involves keeping tabs on percentage of revenues derived from new products and services introduced in the last two to five years, there are many other metrics that spell out to units far afield from new product development what is expected. Once such goals are broadly communicated and rewards for achieving milestones are established, the pace of ideas to implementation accelerates. Growth is the result.

Principle 3: Innovation Must Include an Organized, Systematic, and Continual Search for New Opportunities

Back in the early 1990s, AT&T's top brass allowed a small unit of its planning department to call itself the Opportunity Discovery Department—ODD, for short. This band of maverick thinkers gave itself the task of shaking up the giant company's thinking. One day in 1995, members of the unit donned sandwich boards that read: "What if long distance were free?"

While the question was dismissed as "ridiculous and irrelevant" at the time, five years later the firm's long-distance revenue was declining so rapidly that the company sought to sell off its long-distance unit at fire sale prices. Clearly, today's seemingly irrelevant question could quickly become tomorrow's threat—or opportunity.

Given the torrid pace of change, the rapid commoditization of products, and the convergence of strategies, firms that rely on yesterday's ideas, yesterday's products, and yesterday's assumptions are clearly vulnerable. This is precisely why firms that make innovation a growth-driving discipline have specific systems and practices in place that help them at the so-called "fuzzy front end" of the innovation process, where future possibilities first come into focus.

Royal Dutch/Shell, through a program called GameChanger, has established a global network of company engineers, researchers, managers, and individual contributors. They scan the horizon for potential discontinuities, seeking to spot where "we can use new technologies to attack an existing industry," in the words of a Shell executive who runs the program in the Chemicals Division in Houston.

GameChanger is Shell's way of regularly asking searching questions such as: What do these developments mean to us? How might we take advantage of them? What threats must we respond to now if we are to turn this change into an opportunity?

As we'll explore in the chapters ahead, innovation-disciplined companies promote a deeper understanding of social, demographic, and technological changes in a continual, systematic search for tomorrow's opportunities. And they use novel techniques, such as applying ethnography and archetype research to gain deeper insights into consumer behavior, to give them an edge in exploring implications and opportunities hidden in such trends.

Principle 4: Innovation Must Involve Everyone in the Organization

In most organizations today, new ideas are almost always directed from the top down, rather than from the bottom up. Not only do most organizations not expect their people to innovate; they don't really expect them to think. Nearly two-thirds of the managers and workers surveyed by Kepner-Tregoe, a leading training and consulting firm, said their companies don't use even half their brainpower. More than 70 percent compared their organizations to a "slow moving truck," blaming the condition on a failure to involve employees in decisions and a lack of training or rewards.

Beyond a seldom-used suggestion system for cost-saving ideas, most companies have no way to stimulate or harvest the good ideas of their people. Not so at companies that are designed for continuous, all-enterprise innovation. The assumption that lower-ranked managers and rank and file employees cannot come up with powerful, growth-producing, breakthrough ideas is viewed in these firms as a paradigm unfitted to 21st century reality.

Some Dana Corporation's plants receive four ideas per month, per employee, with a 75 percent implementation rate. At Disney, a thrice-yearly Gong Show, where anyone in the company can pitch a new concept, is the forum where the company's retail format was first proposed by an employee.

At London-based Virgin Group, Ailsa Petchey, a flight attendant who didn't like how she was treated in planning her own wedding, recognized the opportunity to provide a one-stop wedding planning service for busy people. She pitched the idea through the company's Speak Up Program and is today the CEO of a new company division, Virgin Bride. Other firms, such as Siemens and EDS, have put in place global idea networks and sophisticated intranets that plumb the far reaches of the organization for new products and service possibilities.

Not all ideas will be useful. Some will be redundant, self-serving, and trivial. But firms that invest in building an innovation capability, and what have come to be called "idea management systems" to capture ideas, have discovered that this dormant creative potential can be awakened, managed, and translated into a new tool for driving growth.

Principle 5: Innovation Must Be Customer-Centered

Innovation-adept firms live and breathe the customer. They know that the customer is fickle, whimsical, and always difficult to predict, but they don't let that stop them from trying. They also know that creating value for the customer is the only route to success, and that while you can fool some customers all the time, and all customers some of the time, ultimately, the reputation and acceptance of "new and improved" products, services, and service offerings had better deliver.

Because today's customer is more sophisticated, with more information available at the touch of a keyboard to compare and contrast an ever-increasing array of value propositions, the discipline of innovation means learning to listen to customers and potential customers in new ways. And it means inviting the voice of the customer to permeate the design and implementation of new concepts, if those ideas are ultimately going to drive growth.

Structure of the Book

Each of the chapters ahead will integrate these five essential principles of 21st century innovation:

- Approaching innovation as a discipline

- Making it the responsibility of all business units and departments

- Being systematic about discovering future opportunities

- Involving everyone in the process

- Making innovation customer-focused

Each chapter will give you a series of questions to use as you consider, and in some cases upgrade and redesign, your firm's overall approach to innovation. Here's what you'll find in specific chapters of this book:

In Chapter 1, "21st Century Innovation" you'll see why the Growth Gap can't be closed by traditional methods, how innovation can be categorized by type and level, and how some companies in the Vanguard are transforming their futures via an all-enterprise approach to innovation.

In Chapter 2, "Leading Innovation," we'll focus on the five essentials that a firm's top managers must wrestle with if innovation is to become an embedded, growth-driving process. These essentials include the need to define and commit to an innovation strategy; the need to spread responsibility; the need to properly allocate resources; the need to measure innovative progress; and the need to reward and recognize innovation success.

Next, in Chapter 3, "Creating the Culture," we'll address the single most important factor that leadership must shape if it is to deliver a steady stream of innovations: your company's culture. Be forewarned: this chapter will invite you to look at some very pointed aspects of your company's culture. For example, what happens to creative, out-of-the-box mavericks in your organization? What happens when someone fails? The key take-away from this chapter will be suggestions and ideas in how to create a climate that encourages and facilitates systematic, all-enterprise involvement in your company, based on the culture as it exists, rather than the one you might wish were prevalent.

If I have an idea and I work for you, what do you want me to do with it? Stumped? You're not alone. Most firms do not have an answer to this question. Chapter 4, "Empowering the Idea Management Process," helps you and your organization design and implement an idea management system. Without one, you may never hear about potential breakthroughs. Worse, that creative employee in your firm who has a "big one" may take it to another company—possibly his or her own. This chapter provides eight distinct models of idea management, from Citigroup's highly successful Innovation Catalyst Model to Whirlpool's Innovation Team approach, which you can use to develop a process that best suits your needs.

Do you sometimes feel your organization is not looking out ahead often enough, nor far enough? Chapter 5, "Mining the Future," will give you six powerful new ways to visualize the future of your customers and overall market, with an eye toward positioning your company to invent a bigger future. We'll go behind the scenes inside Innovation Vanguard firms that are leading the way in developing new capabilities that help them anticipate tomorrow's environments, maximize their positions, and strategically decide when it's best to move first or follow fast.

What do you do after having immersed yourself in the future to seek out potential breakthroughs? Most firms can improve this "fuzzy front end" of the innovation process, and Chapter 6, "Fortifying the Idea Factory," gives you seven guidelines for how to go about it.

Indeed, if there's one arena where leading companies are currently "innovating how they innovate," it's this one. Innovation Vanguard companies are going beyond the conventional methods of market research, focus groups, and customer surveys to completely redesign their ideational processes. Case examples reported here show how a leading pharmaceutical firm, a global financial services company, and a golf club manufacturer all discovered breakthrough ideas by activating the creativity of their employee base, listening to "lead users," and delving more deeply into their customers' unarticulated needs, wants, and desires.

Chapter 7, "Producing Powerful Products," provides you with an inside look at companies that have redesigned their product development process to drive growth. You will gain familiarity with six powerful methods you can use to improve your firm's batting average with new products. It reports on compelling new research showing how innovation-adept firms contrast with average companies in how they conceptualize, design, and launch new products for growth and profitability.

As Chapter 8, "Generating Growth Strategies," makes clear, no matter how seemingly bulletproof your firm's current business model, it will be challenged by new ones. Over time, it will be imitated, and thereby diluted and commoditized. Upstart competitors may or may not have staying power, yet collectively they can render today's method of creating value for customers passé. This chapter argues that strategy innovation is just as important as product or process innovation and is first and foremost an act of imagination: the ability to see how something could work better from the customer's standpoint, in a way that in turn profits the sponsoring firm. This chapter outlines six ways to jump-start your search for imaginative new business models for your firm.

Chapter 9, "Selling New Ideas," addresses the final, yet essential issue of successful innovation: Can you sell it? No matter how strong an idea, you and your company must be equally skilled at convincing, converting, cajoling, and otherwise creatively "building the buy-in" for new ideas with employees, customers, suppliers, and other stakeholders. This chapter discusses seven powerful strategies to hone your selling skills and will give you some of the success secrets from the innovators behind some of today's biggest breakthroughs.

Finally, Chapter 10, "Taking Action in Your Firm," will help you further assess all the ideas you've gained from reading this book and prioritize the steps to take to implement them.

What This Book Can Do For You

Whether you're the CEO, a general manager, a project manager, a sales and marketing executive, or an individual contributor interested in your firm's future, this book asks you a question and offers you a choice.

The question is straightforward: Are you satisfied with how your company obtains growth and with your present growth rates? If your answer is yes, you may not need this book. But if you see room for improvement, the choice is about what role you'll play. Are you ready to undertake a rethinking of how your company innovates? *Driving Growth Through Innovation* will give you the information you need to organize and lead an initiative in your company that will change how you approach innovation.

As you read the chapters ahead and ponder the questions each one poses, you'll have the opportunity to write a first draft of an innovation strategy that is uniquely right for your firm. As you read about firms that have already taken steps to rev up their growth engines, you'll not only gain a better perspective on the rapidly evolving field of innovation work, you'll get ideas you can use to design a 21st century Innovation Blueprint that's right for your firm.

CHAPTER 1

21st Century Innovation

At the end of the day, what's going to drive our business
is top line growth, so innovation is vital to our future.

—Victor Menezes, Senior Vice Chairman, Citigroup, Inc.

There's an unmistakable feeling of excitement in the air in companies that are growing. People move about with a palpable sense of
purpose. The smiles are brighter, the handshakes firmer. Peer in on
meetings and you see unbridled enthusiasm and passion.

No wonder. Growth in revenue and net earnings begets many
wonderful, positive things to companies and their people. Growth
brings prosperity: higher salaries and bonuses and stock options and
fringe benefits for employees and managers, and dividends and ris-
ing value to investors. Growth brings admiration and respect from
peers and competitors in your industry, from the business media,
and from suppliers and stakeholders. It means being able to give
back to the communities in which the company operates.

Growth means freedom: freedom from the frustration and agony
of having to make difficult choices, of cutting staff, of watching

credit ratings be downgraded, of painful pay cuts. Growth means you control your destiny.

Growth means being able to attract and retain talented people—the best in the industry—and means working in an environment in which everyone can realize his or her potential, achieve promotions, take on new challenges. Growth means winning, and having fun while you are at it!

The vast majority of firms today are growing. Problem is, they aren't growing fast enough to keep up with today's shareholder values, nor tomorrow's shareholder expectations. Higher rates of growth may be desired, but they certainly aren't common. Call it the Growth Gap. Let's take a closer look.

The Growing Growth Gap

A Corporate Strategy Board study analyzed 3700 U.S.-based and non–U.S.-based companies with half a billion dollars or greater in revenues. Of these, only 3.3 percent showed consistent profitable top- and bottom-line growth, and shareholder returns for the seven-year time period analyzed. Only 21 of the 3700 companies, or less than 1 percent, had sustained this growth over the last 20 years. These 21 highly successful growth companies outperformed the S&P during the same time period, with a 26 percent compound annual market cap growth versus 13 percent for the average Standard & Poors companies.

What about the other companies, those that did not enjoy such sustained growth? They came face to face with the Growth Gap, and most responded with methods that had worked in the past.

Why Traditional Methods Won't Close the Gap

Most companies today face their own version of the Growth Gap and are addressing it through traditional means. But the Growth Gap can't be closed by traditional means, which include:

- *Beefing up marketing and sales.*
  A winning advertising campaign can boost sales, increase market share, and drive revenue momentum. But ultimately, marketing can't induce consumers to brush their teeth, shampoo their hair, or wash their dishes more frequently than they already do.

- *Your industry's natural growth rate.*
  Unless you make the latest fad product, your industry's natural rate of growth is probably somewhere close to the growth rate of your country's Gross Domestic Product. Even if you make cellular phones or personal digital assistants, how long will this industry growth continue? These days, the cycle time from industry hypergrowth to industry maturity is shorter, no longer decades, but a finite number of years. Can you really count on your industry's growth rate to fuel your own?

- *Cost-cutting, efficiency-enhancing initiatives.*
  Such efforts are essential to improve a company's bottom line because they increase the spread between gross and net. Companies have spent the past two decades driving costs out of their operations: cutting staff, consolidating operations, introducing a myriad of new technologies. Yet such efforts have not and will not increase top-line revenue, therefore they cannot fuel revenue growth.

- *The traditional new product/service pipeline.*
  This pipeline is very good at developing line extensions and product enhancements. Such linear development occasionally, unexpectedly brings forth a winning new product or service, but for the most part it creates slight variations on a theme, that barely move the growth needle. Clearly, this isn't the way to bridge the Growth Gap.

- *Acquisitions and mergers.*
  Many large companies already buy a dozen or more smaller firms each year as a matter of strategic routine. Many others have attempted mergers of behemoths. Yet this acquisitiveness does not come without risk. The risk of the mergers and acquisitions remedy is in digesting the elephants that the company has gobbled up, melding often incompatible cultures, overcoming regulatory and shareholder objections, avoiding the drain on management's attention, and avoiding the acquisition or merger becoming a drain on profits, as so often happens. Just 23 percent of acquisitions earn their cost of capital, according to a study by consultants at McKinsey, who looked at deals made by 116 companies over an 11-year period. That means the staggering prices

paid to capture other firms often lower growth rates rather than increasing them. Closing the Growth Gap using these traditional measures won't work. What will? Innovation.

Innovation: Key Driver of Growth & Profitability

A landmark study conducted by PricewaterhouseCoopers' British unit demonstrates and documents what members of the Innovation Movement have long been saying: Firms that master innovation are firms that are faster than their peers and produce higher profits.

In analyzing the financial results of 399 companies based in seven countries, PWC found a growth chasm that was most pronounced between the most and least innovative companies. Most innovative were those firms that generated well above average total shareholder returns (greater than 37 percent total shareholder returns annually), and also had more than 75 percent turnover from products and services introduced within the last five years. The study found that:

- The proportion of new products and services is a key indicator of corporate success both in terms of revenue enhancement and total shareholder returns.

- There is a major gap between high and low performers. High performers average 61 percent of turnover from new products as compared to 26 percent for low performers. (Average for this seven-country sample was 38 percent of turnover from new products and services.)

- Nearly a quarter of all companies were generating 10 percent or less of their turnover from new products and services. Growthwise, they have stagnated.

The implications of this study are clear. High-growth firms do a lot of innovating, while low-growth firms do little or none of it. High-growth firms obsolete themselves by coming out with new products and services and entering new markets; low-growth firms do not. Consider:

- Medtronic Corporation typically derives 70 percent of revenues from products introduced during the previous two years.

Company officials are quick to point out that most are either incremental or significant improvements to existing products, such as a next-generation pacemaker that adds an oxygen sensor, rather than a "new to the world" product such as the Parkinson's implant device the company introduced in 2000.

- Colgate-Palmolive receives 38 percent of its revenues from products launched in the last five years, up from 27 percent four years ago.

- Citigroup's best-performing businesses routinely generate 15 to 20 percent of revenue from products that have been introduced in the previous two years.

PWC's research provides evidence for action to those leaders who are determined to tackle the Growth Gap inside their firms. Take two companies with equal revenues and growth rates in the marketplace today. Then, one of them—yours—fundamentally changes how it goes about innovation and begins to increase the introduction of meaningful new products and services.

Over time, observes the report, your company is likely to benefit from a higher growth rate than the other. On average, a 10 percent increase in the percentage of new products and services is correlated with a 2.5 percent increase in the rate of revenue growth.

Recognizing the Role of Innovation

Various surveys indicate that managers and senior executives are already well aware of what the PWC research proves: that innovation has the power to fuel growth. Survey after survey shows strong agreement that, as one termed it, "innovation in our company is viewed as a much more critical business success factor than it was just five years ago."

The Washington D.C.-based Industrial Research Institute counts among its members the chief research and development leaders of the largest U.S. firms. Each year the Institute asks members to name their biggest issues and challenges. In a recent annual survey, "accelerating innovation" and "managing R&D for business growth" clearly dominated, with 37 percent of respondents. Five years earlier, these concerns received only 12 percent of responses. Further, a 1993 study by Synectics Corporation of 750 executives at 150 U.S. companies showed that 80 percent agreed "that innovation is critical to my company's survival and success." Yet only 4 percent indicated their firms were "adept at innovation."

"Despite the acknowledged importance of innovation, less than 25 percent of the responding companies feel that their innovation performance is where it needs to be to succeed in the competitive marketplace," according to an Arthur D. Little survey of 669 global business leaders.

Clearly it's not a question of realization but one of doing something about the realization. While happy accidents can drive growth, it's best to have a Plan B in place. To win the growth game, a growing number of companies are embarking on widespread initiatives to *innovate how they innovate,* and their results so far, are outstanding.

Before we begin to benchmark what these leading firms are doing to transform their future, we need to define what innovation is—and what it is not.

A Simple Definition of Innovation: "Bringing New Ideas to Life"

In its simplest definition, innovation is coming up with ideas and bringing them to life. Hatching ideas is the "creative" part, and it's essential. After all, no ideas, no chance for innovation. Often, in common parlance, the words *creativity* and *innovation* are used interchangeably. They shouldn't be, because while creativity implies coming up with ideas, it's the "bringing ideas to life" piece of this simple definition that makes innovation the distinct undertaking it is.

The Purpose of Innovation: Create New Customer-Perceived Value

To drive growth via innovation requires that your idea do something to benefit customers: create new value. Value encompasses the quality and uniqueness of the product or service, and the degree to which it satisfies the customer's need or problem. Value is also the customer service and add-on services provided as part of the sale, together with the price of the offering or service.

The purpose of innovation is to create new customer-perceived value. If customers perceive value in your new offering, they'll pay you for it. This is the challenge companies face with respect to inno-

Happy Accidents

Happy accident or serendipity has played a role in many an innovation. And there is a body of evidence that gives hope. Nutrasweet, today a $2 billion a year product for G.D. Searle Company, was discovered by a researcher attempting to find a drug to treat ulcers. Pfizer Pharmaceutical's latest blockbuster drug was "accidentally" discovered by scientists attempting to stimulate receptors in the hearts of people with angina. Instead, it was discovered receptors were stimulated elsewhere in the male anatomy, and Viagra in turn stimulated tremendous growth at Pfizer. Canon's ink jet printer was discovered when a technician left a soldering iron on near a bottle of ink. Scotchgard, a breakthrough 3M product since removed from the market on environmental concerns, came about when an employee spilled a substance on her canvas shoe and days later noticed how the spot both repelled liquids and deflected dirt.

vation: How do we develop ideas that indeed create new value for our customers?

Before we address that question, we need to further differentiate the types and degrees of innovation.

The Three Types of Innovation

The matrix in Figure 1 on the next page shows the three types of innovation: product, process, and strategy. In the highly competitive, rapidly evolving environment of the 21st century, achieving rates of growth that are uncommon in your industry means that you must be able to manage innovation in these three distinct arenas. Each arena is critical, and being adept in only one of them is likely not sufficient to achieve the growth payoff from innovation. Let's take a careful look at these arenas.

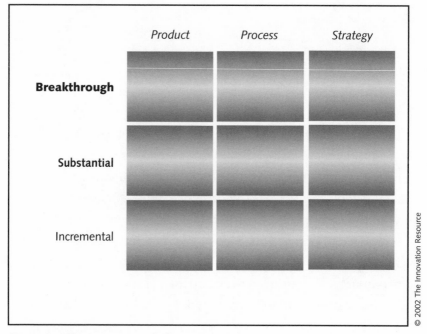

Figure 1   The Innovation Opportunity Grid

Type 1: Product Innovation

Products have traditionally been defined as tangible, physical goods or raw materials ranging from toothpaste to steel beams, from computers to industrial adhesives, from jet aircraft to automobiles to soybeans. All the objects around you at this moment that were manufactured by a company constitute products.

But to confuse matters a bit, in recent years, service sector firms (healthcare, insurance, financial services, professional services, to name only a few) have begun to refer to their offerings as "products" as well. When Merrill Lynch introduced its highly successful Cash Management Account in the early 1980s, this "product" vaulted this service company to the top of its industry.

Adding to the breakdown in traditional boundaries, product manufacturers increasingly surround their products with services, for instance, when car manufacturers offer emergency roadside assistance. General Motors sells cars, but customers buy certain of its automobiles with services as part of the deal. OnStar, an onboard global positioning satellite-enabled communication channel, gives GM customers the ability to know exactly where on Earth they are, and to summon emergency help if they need it.

Despite the recent trend of service firms and manufacturers alike to use the term *products* to describe their offerings, services and service businesses "products" tend to be different. Foremost among them, they can often be intangible as opposed to tangible and physical (an insurance policy as opposed to a snowboard). They also tend to be produced and consumed at the same time and to involve a higher degree of human involvement in their delivery (think healthcare and hospitality). And they tend to be difficult or impossible to stop imitation through the use of patents.

So while there are differences, products and services have common traits, especially when it comes to the subject of innovation. We will use the term *products* to describe the offerings of both types of firms.

And now for the definition: Product/service innovation is the result of bringing to life a new way to solve the customer's problem that benefits both the customer and the sponsoring company.

Type 2: Process Innovation

Process innovations increase bottom-line profitability, reduce costs, raise productivity, and increase employee job satisfaction. The customer also benefits from this type of innovation by virtue of a stronger, more consistent product or service value delivery. The unique trait about process innovations is that they are most often out of view of the customer; they are "back office." Only when a firm's processes fail to enable the firm to deliver the product or service expected does the customer become aware of the lack of effective process.

For manufacturing companies, process innovations include such things as integrating new manufacturing methods and technologies that lead to advantages in cost, quality, cycle time, development time, speed of delivery, or ability to mass-customize products, and services that are sold with those products. Such innovation is important and will continue to be.

Process innovations enable service firms to introduce "front office" customer service improvements and add new services, as well as new "products" that are visible to the customer. When FedEx introduced its unique tracking system in 1986, customers saw only a tiny wand, used by drivers to scan packages. Yet while the rest of this sophisticated system was invisible, customers could "see" immediately that they could now track their packages at every point from sender to receiver, and this added value to their service experience and gave Federal Express a temporary advantage.

Process innovation will continue to be vitally important to company growth for the simple reason that without process excellence, product or strategy innovation is impossible to implement. Indeed, while thousands of books have been written about varying methods of process improvement (read, innovation), the innovation process, unlike say the product development process, is untrammeled territory. That's why the innovation process itself is, in essence, the subject of this book.

Type 3: Strategy Innovation

Strategy innovation is about challenging existing industry methods of creating customer value in order to meet newly emerging customer needs, add additional value, and create new markets and new customer groups for the sponsoring company.

In contrast to process innovations, which are "behind the scenes" and largely unseen by the customer, strategy innovations directly touch the customer.

Strategy innovation results in new approaches to marketing or advertising your offerings, in introducing new sales methods, and in new approaches or enhancements to customer service or market positioning. Strategy innovation results when your firm changes the customer groups it targets and how it "goes to market," meaning how it distributes its offerings to end customers (Figure 2).

A key element of strategy innovation occurs when a firm decides to market its existing products, services, or expertise to new customer groups. That's what defense contractor Hughes Electronics did when it began its DirecTV division in the early 1990s, using its expertise with satellites to begin beaming cable channels and movies to home satellite dishes. More commonly, when a firm such as a traditional retailer decides to additionally sell its wares via the web, that's strategy innovation.

Much of the highly visible innovation occurring in business today is strategy innovation, and much, but no means all of it

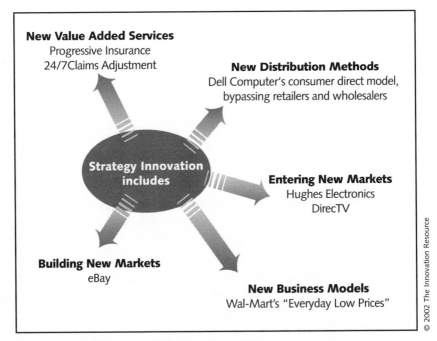

New Value Added Services
Progressive Insurance
24/7Claims Adjustment

New Distribution Methods
Dell Computer's consumer direct model,
bypassing retailers and wholesalers

Strategy Innovation includes

Entering New Markets
Hughes Electronics
DirecTV

Building New Markets
eBay

New Business Models
Wal-Mart's "Everyday Low Prices"

Figure 2   The Elements of Strategy Innovation

involves the exploitation of new technology. Dell Computer's very business model is a prime example of strategy innovation because it represents a dramatically different way of manufacturing and selling personal computers. Dell chose not to distribute its products through the then-standard channel—to wholesalers or resellers, who sold to retailers, who then sold to end-customers. Instead Dell sold directly to end-customers.

Other innovations rounding out Dell's contrary business model were strategic in nature as well: From the beginning, Dell didn't manufacture a single computer until it received a customer's order. And the product was then manufactured to order, rather than creating an inventory of standardized products to be stored until sold in one warehouse or another.

Similarly, firms ranging from eBay to Amazon.com represent strategy innovations when compared to the way their respective industries traditionally did business. While these and many other strategy innovations relied on technology to change the game, not all strategy innovation is based on technology.

Southwest Airlines was a strategy innovator in the airline business. Its business model is based on offering customers low fares in exchange for their giving up such amenities as preassigned seating, meals, nonstop flights, the ability to book using a travel agent, and other value-added services—all aspects of Southwest's business model that differed from competitors.

Price Club, which later merged with Costco, pioneered warehouse club retailing, a strategy innovation. "Category killers" with names like Office Depot, Home Depot, Staples, Borders, Petsmart, IKEA, and CompUSA, all pioneered new business models in their time. Traditional merchants were caught flat-footed in the 1980s when Wal-Mart pioneered a new business model, and customers began voting for what they perceived to be a superior value proposition, killing off traditional competitors. Wal-Mart and others offered many of the same products as traditional merchants, but offered everyday low pricing to lure customers with a perception of greater value. As a result of their success, many traditional department stores and merchants were forced out of business.

Not All Innovations Jump-start Growth

Not all innovations in these three arenas accelerate growth to the same extent. The degree to which an innovation adds value or creates new value for customers is the degree to which it adds to a company's bottom line. What innovation-adept companies strive for, in addition to ongoing processes that keep the pipeline full, are high-potential ideas in each of these arenas. Ideas that change the game. Ideas that change the rules of competition. Ideas that move the growth needle!

Not all innovations, of course, have an equal impact on customers, and certainly not on a company's rate of growth or wealth-creating ability. All product, process, and strategy innovations can be categorized further into three basic degrees: incremental, substantial, and breakthrough (Figure 3).

Incremental Innovation

While small or even insignificant in degree of financial impact to the firm's bottom line, incremental improvements can engender greater customer satisfaction, increase product or service efficacy and other-

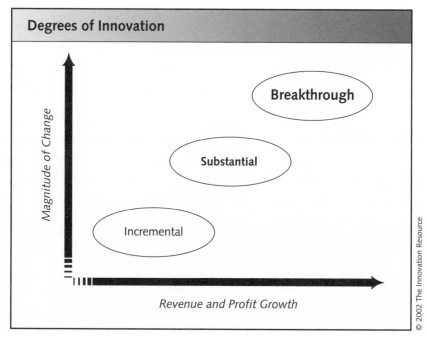

Figure 3   Not all innovations have equal impact on revenue and profit growth. Breakthrough innovations are most significant in this respect, although they often require the greatest amount of change, internally and externally, to implement.

wise have positive impact. Similarly, process innovations of incremental degree increase productivity and lower cost for the firm.

Incremental innovations have this in common: They seldom require more than minor changes in customer or company behavior to implement. 3M's introduction of a new color Post-it® Note qualifies as an incremental product innovation, while Post-it Notes represented a breakthrough product innovation. Implementing a suggestion program—a process innovation—requires employees to change behavior very little since submitting ideas is optional.

In the service sector, incremental innovation occurs when a hotel simplifies its guest check-in procedure; a supermarket chain makes check approval easier than summoning the manager; a bank redecorates its lobby; a retirement home upgrades signage to address seniors' failing eyesight; an international airline upgrades its first-class cabin to include fully reclining sleeper seats.

Incremental process innovation has gotten a bad rap in recent years on the assumption that incrementalism is the enemy of genuine innovation. One reason for this is that in many firms, incremental innovation has replaced the quest for more significant innovation—those that add more value to customers, and as a result, bolster the business accordingly. Incremental innovations are often quickly matched by competitors, which cancel out any "first mover" benefit to the initiating firm's bottom line. Worse, if a firm is spending its time thinking merely about incremental innovation, it probably isn't spending time reinventing the product category or attacking its own value proposition with a radically improved one.

Constant improvements are essential to companies engaged in pioneering new markets or rolling out radically different products. They know that thousands upon thousands of incremental innovations are a necessary and beneficial part of the process. So incrementalism is a good and necessary endeavor, and needs to be supported. But the cumulative effect of incrementalism without vision is that a company stops inventing its future with radically better products and services and markets.

Substantial Innovations

Substantial innovations are mid-level in significance both to customers who benefit from them and to the sponsoring company that believes they will significantly help the firm grow and create new wealth. Substantial innovations of the product/service variety fall short of being breakthroughs, but enable and ensure that the organization meets or exceeds its goals to grow the business, increase market share, and lower its cost of doing business (substantial-level process innovation).

Substantial improvements in your existing products and services or introducing new-to-the company products and services represent significant improvements for both the service providing company and for the customer.

Breakthrough Innovations

New products, services, or alterations of your strategy that yield a significant increase in revenues and net profits are breakthrough innovations. It is impossible to define in dollars and cents how much revenue an idea must bring to the top line to classify as a breakthrough

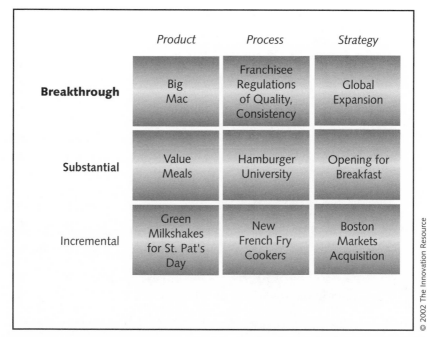

	Product	Process	Strategy
Breakthrough	Big Mac	Franchisee Regulations of Quality, Consistency	Global Expansion
Substantial	Value Meals	Hamburger University	Opening for Breakfast
Incremental	Green Milkshakes for St. Pat's Day	New French Fry Cookers	Boston Markets Acquisition

Figure 4   McDonald's Corporation has innovated successfully in each of the important parts of the grid. As an exercise, try filling out this grid for your company.

because it depends on the size of your company and what it takes to significantly drive growth. So, breakthroughs must be self-defined, but need to be if you are serious about going after them. When we asked how large an idea had to be to be designated a breakthrough at the Chemicals Division of Royal Dutch/Shell, the answer was $100 million or more to the top line.

Process improvements that generate a significant reduction in costs or an equivalent increase in productive output are also breakthroughs.

Breakthrough inventions can sometimes lead to breakthrough-level innovations for numerous companies. Breakthrough inventions are giant leaps forward for humankind that lack proprietary parents and may not provide "first mover advantage" to a single company, but instead spawn an entire new industry.

The automobile, the invention of electricity, the discovery of penicillin, the Internet, and the World Wide Web are all breakthrough

Radical Innovations

Radical innovations are those that require your company to develop a whole new business or product line based on new ideas or technologies or cost reductions, and that transform the economics of the sponsoring business and disrupt entire industries.

The important point is that not all radical innovations become breakthrough innovations, and not all breakthrough innovations are radical. Radical innovations that become breakthroughs provide customers whole new ways of solving their problems or meeting their needs, and in some cases they actually create new needs. Moreover, they require the sponsoring firm to be a first mover, or at least a fast follower, a subject about which we'll have more to say in a later chapter.

When you analyze breakthrough ideas, you find that some are radical innovations. Indeed, in a major study of radical innovations, such as DuPont's biodegradable fiber, GE's digital X-ray system, and others, a team of Rensselaer Polytechnic Institute researchers concluded that:

- Radical innovations can be stimulated by concerted effort, as opposed to waiting for happy accidents to occur.
- Radical innovations often take ten or more years to develop into a commercial product and additional time to build the market.
- Radical ideas need to have different processes and funding to guide their development.
- Radical ideas often require multiple champions to see them from idea to implementation.

While we're all for radical innovation, they are not what this book is primarily about. We don't want to wait 15 to 25 years for a payout, and we assume you don't either. Fortunately, many ideas that become breakthroughs are not that radical, or that risky, for that matter.

inventions. While the automobile was a breakthrough in how people transported themselves from place to place, no single company could claim to have benefited exclusively from having invented it or had the legally protected right to market it. And it's the same with the Internet, television, and lots of other products.

On the other hand, some new products, services, processes, and business models *do* have proprietary parents and simultaneously give temporary monopoly to the sponsoring firm—it is this type of innovation that we focus on in this book.

Two Breakthrough Examples

When Gillette, facing intense competition from cheap disposable razors, decided to develop its Sensor shaving system in the early 1990s, the product became a breakthrough almost immediately. Radical innovation? Hardly. The market was familiar—men with whiskers. The product category was familiar too. The innovation came in the strategic decision to go up-market and not compete on price. And it came in the superior value it delivered to the user, and the difficult-to-copy, 22-patent product and marketing campaign that was the result of a billion-dollar investment.

When Volkswagen decided to launch an updated, restyled version of its famous Beetle, which had been discontinued in North American markets due to an inability to meet strict emissions standards in the 1970s, the result was an instant breakthrough for Volkswagen AG. Radical innovation? Hardly. Obvious moves for these two companies? Not at the time.

What about at your company, have you had any breakthroughs lately? Maybe it's time for a new approach—a 21st century approach.

The 21st Century Approach: All-Enterprise Innovation

If 75 percent of today's managers are frustrated and dissatisfied with their firm's innovation performance (according to the Arthur D. Little survey cited earlier), what are the remaining 25 percent doing to bring about results? And what can they teach us that we might apply to our own efforts?

The short answer: plenty! In these firms, the Innovation Vanguard, innovation is no longer approached in traditional ways but is instead approached as an enterprise-wide process, and as a specific, vital discipline. Traditional research and development teams and efforts are not supplanted, but they are supported in fundamentally different ways.

Most companies today—the 75 percent dissatisfied—have no organized, comprehensive system for identifying disruptive changes or for finding the future. This is not the case at innovation-adept companies. Royal Dutch/Shell's divisions have installed sophisticated global disruptive technology units, and fund promising new ideas that embrace "white space" opportunities, those that don't fit neatly into existing business units and require development effort to bring to market.

Most companies today—the 75 percent dissatisfied—have no leading indicators to systematically measure innovation, only lagging indicators to measure past performance. They have no organized approach to cut bureaucracy, or to force people to disengage long enough from the problems and pressures of the present to engage in a dialogue about the future. They don't have a process to turn to that tells them, "be a first mover to exploit this technology," or "fast follower is a better strategy in this instance."

Most companies today leave it to marketing to introduce, launch, and sell their new ideas into the marketplace. No matter how new, they rely on a department to get the job done. And what happens? Consumer products makers cranked out 31,000 new products in a recent year alone, but few of these products will create top-line revenue growth, and few will survive. This is decidedly not the case at Innovation Vanguard companies.

Every year, *Business Week* magazine compiles its list of growth champions, some of which have doubled their size in the previous year. While we salute these hard chargers in their endeavors, these are not the companies we studied. Johnson & Johnson is hardly a dot-com, nor is it growing at 300 percent a year. Johnson & Johnson is a highly decentralized collection of operating companies that has increased sales more than tenfold over the past two decades, while never once missing a dividend, with a relentless focus on innovation.

Kimberly-Clark could easily have convinced itself that it was in a mature market and attempted to get shareholders to lower their expectations. But that's not what the Dallas-based company did, as we'll see in later chapters.

In these firms, the approach to innovation is comprehensive—it changes how every department and business unit does its work. It is driven by CEOs and business unit heads that don't simply give lip service to the importance of innovation—they passionately support it through goals and metrics and rewards and resources. These CEOs appoint senior managers to be in charge of seeing that it happens, and they reward and recognize its occurrence.

In these companies, the search for growth-spawning big ideas is dramatically different. It is organized and ongoing and often embraces unconventional techniques (as described in later chapters) to get closer to as yet unarticulated customer needs and to "suss out" future opportunities.

Perhaps the most predominant trait of these companies is their broad-based cultural commitment to bottoms-up innovation to carry out the top-down strategic growth goals set by senior management.

These firms realize well that to accelerate growth means to accelerate innovation, and to accelerate innovation means accelerating idea development and implementation. Ideas, no matter their source of origin, are managed in new and innovative ways that ensure that more ideas will ultimately lead to better ideas; and better ideas at every step of the development process will lead to a better batting average of successful launches, and products, services, processes, and strategic alterations that impact the firm's top and bottom lines.

But enough with such generalizations; let's go inside a leading financial services firm that allowed us to study its practice of innovation.

Citigroup's New Approach to Driving Growth Through Innovation

Citigroup was formed in 1998 as the result of a merger between Citicorp, the global corporate and consumer bank, and The Travelers Group. Long known for its growth through acquisitions, Citigroup sought to balance those acquisitions with organic growth, which had taken a back seat during the merger and subsequent large acquisitions. Senior managers also saw that it could be doing a lot more to enhance revenue momentum by simply encouraging cross-selling of products between business units, and between and among the many countries in which it operates.

By objective measures, Citigroup's reputation was already that of a highly-rated innovative company. In the year it launched the Global Innovation Initiative, it ranked third in Fortune magazine's annual survey of corporate reputations for overall innovativeness, trailing only now bankrupt Enron and Charles Schwab among other U.S.-based corporations, and number one by a significant margin in the banking industry.

But true to form, Citigroup's top brass wasn't satisfied with leaving well enough alone. Victor Menezes, chairman and CEO of Citibank NA and head of Citigroup's Emerging Markets Division, was looking for a way to more than double net income every five years in emerging markets. Given such aggressive targets, there was no time to waste. "At the end of the day," Menezes told his management team, "what's going to drive our business is top-line revenue growth, and that means innovation in terms of new products, new processes, new business models, and new services."

In 2000, Menezes made the decision to undertake a fundamental redesign of Citigroup's innovation process. He appointed a 30-person task force of bright up-and-comers from throughout the far-flung organization, encouraged them to benchmark companies that already had exemplary innovation processes in place, and see what they could find out. He also urged them to listen anew to Citigroup's myriad customers for their ideas and input, and to meet with internal players to solicit their input on what the bank wasn't doing well to translate good ideas into revenue growth.

Answering these objectives led the group, which gave itself the name Team Challenge 2000, to fan out for site visits with innovators at companies such as Electronic Data Service (EDS), Caterpillar, and 3M. They interviewed innovation veterans and asked tough questions about barriers to innovation in the global organization. They found widespread agreement inside their own organization that the approval process for new ideas was bureaucratic and slow, that cycle time for introducing new ideas was too long, that the bank was excessively risk-averse.

In addition, Citigroup assessed itself as not being good enough at identifying customer needs, its operations and technology function was said to be too slow to implement in an "Internet world," the firm lacked idea champions, and there was insufficient "multifunctional involvement across stages of product development."

The team also saw that the firm's Citibank unit had a long history of innovation upon which to build. They scouted out what they termed "pockets of extraordinary performance" as well. They found exemplary innovation processes in places like Hong Kong and Brazil— the latter had completely revamped its approach three years earlier and was showing impressive results. In the end, Team Challenge 2000 produced a report that laid out how the company could proceed to foster innovation from every unit and division in the organization.

Among its key recommendations, the task force urged that an innovation initiative be launched, suggesting that it would be best to start on the corporate and consumer banking side in emerging market countries. In addition, it should align with the highly decentralized structure of the organization, which operates in 102 countries.

Another finding was that tremendous top-line momentum could be achieved simply by getting individual countries to learn about and adopt the good ideas that were already generating revenues in other Citibank locales. Under the present decentralized arrangement, if Singapore happened to have invented a banking product that was showing great gains, Venezuela or Poland might not even have heard about the success. Enhancing communication regarding winning new products and services was a major tenet of the initiative's design.

Its key recommendation was that, to successfully embed innovation into the very fiber of the organization, a steering committee of key regional leaders would be necessary, and Menezes tapped Jorge Bermudez, a 26-year veteran with the firm, and chief of the bank's e-business unit, to oversee implementation while still heading up e-business. Bermudez handpicked a far-flung team (called the Network) to help steer implementation and recruited Claus Friis, a former member of Menezes' strategy team, to come aboard as a full-time manager of the initiative.

At the kickoff meeting, Bermudez told the Network, "Our role as catalysts is not to make innovation happen, but to facilitate its occurrence within line businesses and in key business functions. Our role is to knock down the barriers that exist, to take advantage of the diversity of the bank, and to put a process in place that embeds innovation in such a way as to drive revenue growth. We should not expect this to be easy. We should expect 'push back' [resistance], and we should force ourselves to do this without setting up a bureaucracy."

At the heart of the Innovation Initiative was putting the right metrics in place. The Citibank Division already had an Innovation Index in place that measured revenues derived from new products, but that was deemed insufficient. Bermudez challenged the Network to come up with more meaningful top-line metrics that could be used to track progress and could be integrated into the balanced scorecard, and ultimately tied to compensation of senior managers. The team eventually settled on 12 key metrics. They included such things as: new revenue from innovation, success transfer of products from one country or region to another, the number and type of ideas in the pipeline (and expected new revenues), and time from idea to profit.

In the next stage of the rollout, the Network oversaw the appointment of Innovation Catalysts within each country, whose job became that of innovation champion. In a later chapter, we'll look at how these champions drive growth via new products, but let's cut away from the story here for a brief recap.

Designing Your Own 21st Century Innovation Strategy

This book wasn't written for the armchair enthusiast for innovation or the passive observer. You and your firm can enjoy the rewards that Citigroup and other firms now enjoy as a result of acting on their belief that they could get better at innovation. Use this book as a guide in crafting your own innovation strategy, beginning with the issues raised in this chapter.

Rather than turning the page and moving on to Chapter 2, consider the questions below and write down your responses.

- How satisfied are you with your firm's current rate of revenue and net earnings growth?

- How would you describe your firm's current innovation process and are you satisfied that it is the best it can be?

- How do you practice the discipline of innovation, and who in your organization is allowed to participate in this discipline?

- What would it take to rethink your approach to innovation and to roll out an initiative that drives growth?

By pausing to answer the questions posed at the conclusion of each chapter while these issues are fresh in your mind, a vivid picture will emerge of what your organization can look like and how it can function when it is operating with a 21st century innovation strategy in place. For now, don't concern yourself with all the obstacles and barriers that might work against such progress. We'll deal with how to gain "buy-in" for change in later chapters.

Gaining support for an innovation initiative is part of the process. The decision is up to you as to what you do with the insights you'll gain from reading this book. But if you accept the challenge to take action on these ideas, the journey is about to begin.

CHAPTER 2

Leading Innovation

The way we're going to survive is to innovate our way out of this.

Steve Jobs

Founder and Chairman, Apple Computer

Today's leaders face a quandary. They know they must innovate, lest tomorrow the cupboard of new growth opportunities be found bare. But they also know that time is short, especially for the CEO. While executive compensation has zoomed upward in recent years, so too have stakeholder expectations.

"What is striking is not just the number of CEOs getting the boot but how little time they were allowed to prove themselves," noted *Business Week* in a recent cover story. Consider just how fast today's revolving door spins for those at the top:

- Two-thirds of all major companies worldwide replaced their CEO at least once in the last five years, according to a survey by Drake Beam Morin Inc.

- More than 1000 CEOs left office during a recent year.

- CEOs in 39 of the 200 largest U.S. companies left their jobs in a recent year, according to compensation specialists Pearl Meyer & Partners.

The Leader's Preoccupation: Short-Term Results

Unless the CEO is able to raise the company's stock price in the near term, he or she well realizes that they may not be around to see the payoff from projects that are in the development stages right now. This preoccupation with short-term results has led to rampant cost-cutting, asset manipulation, and ill-advised acquisitions. Nevertheless, there is a growing realization among boards of directors, Wall Street analysts, and senior management teams that innovation must be a continuing priority regardless of who sits in the CEO's chair.

The Problem with Visionary Leadership

Some observers argue that the real problem is that Wall Street's expectations of growth are unrealistic. The ability of the CEO to effectuate growth, according to this line of thinking, has been inflated to the point where mortals no longer qualify. This mythologizing of the CEO began in the early 1980s when leaders like Jack Welch of GE and Lee Iacocca of Chrysler, through sheer force of personality and brilliance of vision, not only transformed their companies but carved out incredible results. The problem, though, is that there aren't enough Jack Welches to go around. And many so-called visionaries end up not delivering.

Problems at Bank One

John McCoy was long touted as a visionary who could turn a small bank from Columbus, Ohio, into one of the largest banks in the United States. Indeed, Bank One was often credited with a number of industry firsts. In the 1970s, Bank One was first to be awarded a contract to do the processing for Merrill Lynch's Cash Management Account, the brokerage industry's revolutionary full-service checking and credit-card product.

In the 1980s, Bank One was first to provide online banking to various interactive cable television projects. In the 1990s, Bank One led the acquisitions trend, buying up dozens of small midwestern banks before swallowing giants First Chicago and Valley National in Arizona, among others. The bank proclaimed itself a pioneer in the use of derivatives to hedge interest-rate risks and it was among the first to start an Internet bank, Wingspanbank.com.

Despite all the firsts, McCoy never delivered where it matters most. The bank's stock stayed stagnant, market capitalization remained below average, and growth minus acquisitions was as flat as a Kansas cornfield. Uncommonly patient with McCoy's "just around the corner" promises, the market finally began to ask, if McCoy was so visionary, why wasn't he rich. In 1999, McCoy was forced into retirement by his own hand-picked board.

The Visionary's Blind Spot

Why single out McCoy when history is full of such figures? Some examples:

- Henry Ford told customers they could have any color car they wanted so long as it was black, and the Ford Motor Company took a back seat to General Motors for years as a result.

- Steve Jobs ignored calls to license his Macintosh operating system, only to watch Bill Gates' clunky, inferior system, DOS take over the world, leaving Apple Computer with less than 5 percent of the market.

- Ken Olsen built Digital Equipment Corporation, a company that made minicomputers in the 1980s, bringing the power of computers to the desktop, and thereby to the aid of individual managers. But then he dismissed the trend toward distributed computing, and famously rejected the idea of the personal computer, leading to Digital's decline into takeover bait.

Visionary leaders often go against great odds to sell customers on their ideas and win marketplace acceptance. Search the history of many a great company and you find a leader with a vision of a new product, a better solution for the customer, the creation of a new market.

But their blind spots and personal peccadilloes are legendary as I discovered in researching my first book, *Winning the Innovation Game*, based on interviews with 50 of them. They often surround themselves with "yes" men and are intolerant of dissenting views.

They do not tolerate other equally strong-willed personalities, which is to their detriment in a world that is increasingly complex, fast-changing, and counterintuitive.

Our advice: The "vision thing" is highly overrated. Lack of vision can actually become a positive attribute, so long as you are open-minded and willing to put a process in place to identify opportunities and new markets. Indeed, a willingness to learn more about innovation leadership, and treat it as nothing more than a set of learnable skills, will better serve you in the long run.

The Problem with Administrator Types

Most organizations don't have a visionary at the helm, nor do they have a problem of too much vision. Theirs is just the opposite: too little vision, too much inertia, and an inability to implement quickly in the face of unrelenting change and competition.

Result: Too many leaders are stuck on the "vision thing." They perceive themselves as failures if they do not single-handedly conceive the new strategic initiative, the breakthrough product or service, or the next killer app. This kind of thinking may be the biggest impediment to getting started with a redesign of the firm's innovation process.

You might expect us to be partial to visionary leadership. Actually, we're partial to *having a vision,* but that doesn't mean the vision has to come from the CEO. Ultimately, the problem for companies led by visionaries is the same as for companies led by administrators. Neither has an innovation strategy in place. The visionary leader thinks he *is* the innovation strategy, while the administrator doesn't see the need for one.

Leading in the 21st century calls for executives who can manage the present while concomitantly managing the future. Maintaining focus on consistent execution and short-term results will continue to be the order of the day. But at the same time, firms must ensure that the often overwhelming obligations of day-to-day execution do not crowd out attention being paid to radical shifts in the competitive environment.

To do this, our study of Innovation Vanguard firms finds that they have put processes in place that virtually force them to devote attention and resources to inventing the future. What does this

Five Essentials of Leading Innovation

1. Design and implement an innovation strategy.

2. Spread responsibility for making innovation happen.

3. Allocate resources and decide on levels of risk.

4. Establish innovation metrics.

5. Reward innovation.

process look like? To answer that question, let's turn our attention to designing and building such a process in your firm.

Five Essentials of Leading Innovation

A popular adage in recent management theory goes like this: managing is doing things right, while leading is doing the right things. What are the right things with regard to innovation? The five most important leadership functions in building an all-enterprise innovation capacity are given below.

Leadership Strategy 1:
Design and Implement an Innovation Strategy

An innovation strategy spells out how you intend to embed and systematize innovation in your firm, and how you will turn it into an ongoing, measurable, manageable process. It defines how you will organize the search for tomorrow's opportunities and what is expected of everyone in the organization.

In addition, an innovation strategy describes the kind of culture you intend to establish vis-à-vis innovation. It spells out how innovation will be measured and rewarded, how ideas and proposals will be assessed. In short, it describes your unique approach to innovation, and it puts it in writing for all to see, understand, and use to guide their actions and behavior.

Coming up with such a blueprint can be tasked to the top team, or to an appointed or self-selected team. If the leader is not directly involved in creating this blueprint, it's essential that he or she show ownership and widely endorse the design team's work, and their recommendations, which must be disseminated throughout the organization as coming from the top.

If you are the leader of your organization, you don't have to come up with this strategy yourself. In fact, to try to do so would be a mistake. But you do need to encourage the process and be the catalyst behind its success by virtue of the importance you personally place on it. The role of the leader is to ensure that the strategy gets developed and put in place.

Your innovation strategy should:

- Establish a common definition of what innovation means in your firm.

- Spell out the behaviors you want to encourage.

- Spell out the growth goals your innovation strategy will help you reach.

- Provide a process in every area of the firm to channel people's ideas.

- Outline a plan to overcome your unique organizational barriers to innovation.

- Embed innovation in your organization.

- Appoint a leader to be in charge of innovation.

Let's explore these components of an innovation strategy.

Define Innovation in Your Firm

Articulating a common definition is at the heart of developing an innovation strategy and an excellent starting place for the task force charged with improving innovation capability. In Chapter 1, we defined innovation as product, process, or strategy; nevertheless, your task force will want to define it for your business.

One company defined it as "The freedom to think differently and to create ideas, initiatives, products, and services that add value to current and future business." Another firm, an apparel company, took pains to expand people's past definition as being confined solely to new products or product improvements. "Innovation is the ability and willingness to look at better ways of doing things; new products that improve how people work or live or dress; new, easier, more efficient ways to deliver those products to market; new, more profitable ways to produce or procure those products or run the company."

Do people in your organization know the difference between a breakthrough, a substantial, and an incremental idea? They should. Moreover, it's important to let managers and rank and file employees alike know that they aren't limited in their ideas to merely hatching incremental process improvements. After all, it was a cashier at Home Depot who was responsible for an innovative new inventory control system, a flight attendant at Virgin Atlantic Airlines who came up with the idea to start a new bridal registry company. So it's essential to get everybody in the company to be aware of what breakthrough ideas look like, smell like, and taste like, and the outrageously positive things they do for the company's fortunes.

Your definition of innovation should also indicate your aggressiveness toward breakthroughs or toward incremental innovation. This aggressiveness will depend on your "industry clockspeed"—the rate of change your industry is experiencing and the pace at which products, services, and even business models are becoming obsolete by you or other players in your industry. In addition, your growth goals and strategic plans must be factored in.

Spell Out Behaviors to Encourage   It is not enough to simply give lip service to innovation by altering your mission statement or vision statement. It's essential that everyone in your organization understand what new behaviors and approaches you are calling for.

At one brewing company, when the new CEO took the helm, he appointed a team that made innovation a new value at the company. Associates in the company were encouraged to challenge the status quo, seek to find new ways of doing things, involve a variety of people with diverse backgrounds, and demonstrate advocacy. "Build upon others' ideas and take action on suggestions for improvement. Ensure that others are encouraged and rewarded for expressing different views. Recognize creativity in others."

Spell Out Growth Goals   At Borg-Warner, the goal became growth through innovation in product leadership. Instead of providing ever-cheaper parts for the automotive industry it primarily serves, in 1996 CEO John Fiedler reorganized the company and adopted an innovation strategy. "We're going to become a five billion dollar organization by 2004," Fiedler told his people. "Our goal is to achieve $600 million in new cross-business activity, whether it's engines and transmissions working together or any of our divisions."

In an interview with Alan Bauer, a senior vice-president at Ohio-based Progressive Insurance, we asked him about working for asuccessfully visionary boss, Peter Lewis, who took over a $6 million company from his father, and turned it into a $6 billion concern 20 years later. "Peter always had straightforward objectives for management," Bauer comments. "To grow as fast as possible, always subject to profitability at a given level. We've not grown through category expansion, or through acquisitions, we've grown because Peter urged us to grow through innovation."

Provide a Process to Channel People's Ideas   If managers in your firm today were asked the question: "If I work for you and I have an idea, what do you want me to do with it?" What would their response be? Would they be able to talk about the process with ease and comfort, or would they hem and haw and backpedal? Would they have top-of-mind examples to share? The answer to this issue is to establish an idea management system that is right for your firm, which we'll discuss in Chapter 4: "Empowering the Process."

Plan to Overcome Organizational Barriers to Innovation   Every organization has barriers. These barriers can be internal, having to do with cultural impediments. They can be external, having to do with marketplace resistance to change, costs associated with adopting new ideas, or even barriers springing from resistance from channel partners.

Borg-Warner, under CEO John Fiedler, figured it had to come up with almost a billion dollars in new product ideas to remain a top-tier supplier. The firm hired Baltimore-based Business Innovation Consortium (BIC) led by David Sutherland, an innovation consultant and founder of BIC, to formulate an enterprise-wide process. BIC zeroed in on two organizational barrier issues: (1) No process to deliver new ideas on a consistent basis, and (2) the company's six business units were so autonomous that there was little chance for ideas to bounce back and forth between them.

Sutherland believed that the best way to smoke out barriers (and to devise an innovation strategy) was to galvanize around a high-profile project, overlay a "basis" innovation process, and observe how the system behaves. So the firm organized an Innovation Summit, a three-day idea-fest held in the old Dodge mansion outside Detroit. On the final day of the confab, senior leadership of the $3 billion company showed up to hear presentations of the top four ideas, then retreated to discuss. An hour later, they emerged to endorse one that they funded on the spot and moved into the next steps of the innovation process.

To overcome the "functional and divisional silo" barrier, two company-wide councils were established—one for sales and marketing and one for technical people—that would meet regularly to exchange ideas. Simon Spencer, a senior Borg-Warner engineer, became the first Innovation Champion responsible for leading efforts to improve the company's greatest weakness, coming up with tomorrow's opportunities. Result: Instead of being totally focused on "how many widgets GM, Ford, and Chrysler need," says Spencer, "Borg-Warner is paying greater attention to what lead users are doing and thinking, and intensely studying regulatory bodies for hints about future requirements."

Like Borg-Warner, your company has internal and external barriers that act as friction in its innovation engine. A big part of designing an innovation strategy is properly assessing your internal capabilities, as well as those in the external marketplace, and designing your process to overcome them.

Embed Innovation in Your Organization Any company that wants to complete the task of making innovation a way of life—"the way we do things around here"—needs to launch an innovation initiative. As an initiative, it will have similarities to other initiatives your company has no doubt launched, but will have important differences too.

The quality initiatives, reengineering initiatives, enterprise resource planning initiatives, and many others that companies have launched during the past 20 years give us many insights into successfully launching an innovation initiative. For example, initially, Quality had a special staff with a lot of responsibility and attention from decision makers. Over time, Quality became accepted as part of the baseline responsibilities of each functional area and manager.

Initially, the innovation team is responsible for piloting the initiative in a part of the organization and for training people in the new system. At some point, this responsibility should be shifted to the training office and handled as part of standard practices.

Appoint an Innovation Leader At EDS, Melinda Lockhart is the manager of EDS Innovates. When asked what it takes to succeed in the rollout of an innovation initiative she commented:

> It's energy, passion, strong ability to collaborate and be able to influence things and people that are not under their control. You have to be able to influence the executives. But you also have to be likable and approachable by employees. Someone who is the CEO's fair-haired child may not necessarily be someone who employees can identify with.
>
> You probably don't want to put the person who was in charge of your Quality Initiative in charge, because if that's a role their personality is well adopted to, they may have a rigid mindset, and they're probably not going to be successful in innovation. Innovation is a lot more abstract, so you have to have someone who also deals well with the abstract. A lot of your strategic planning, strategic thinkers are good at that—but [your innovation leader] has got to be able to implement, and therefore, they need an implementation mind-set. It's a rare beast who can have great vision and also implement that vision. You typically have people who are visionary, but are not very effective at implementation. Or they have great implementation skills but someone else has to vision around it. So you need someone, and it's those rare few that are qualified. Innovation leaders have to have an ability to influence, to manage the political landscape.

Finding a willing person to take on the role of innovation catalyst is important in that it tells you a great deal about your company's culture. Is a senior person in the firm willing to devote part-time or full-time to spearheading an innovation initiative? If candidates are hard to come by, what does that tell you about the organization and how such a career move is viewed?

Leadership Strategy 2:
Spread Responsibility for Making Innovation Happen

Leading innovation springs from the realization that it is much too important to be left to the top team. Just as the CEO and his or her senior colleagues can't effectively handle the innovation piece, neither can any department. Instead, leadership must deputize everyone in the organization in the idea-hunting posse, idea-implementing process such that responsibility is diffused throughout the organization.

Ironically, it's the traditional monopolists of innovation—marketing and R&D—who most resent others in the organization getting involved. At one mid-sized New England utility that launched a customized suggestion system, as long as the ideation was confined to incremental process improvements, the marketing department had no problem with "making innovation everyone's responsibility." But they got bent out of shape when the program extended to new products and services the utility might offer customers. Similar squawks were heard from the R&D head at a multinational consumer products company. The purchasing team had attempted to enlarge its mandate to include suggesting new product ideas arising from their partnering relationship with suppliers.

To spread responsibility for embedding innovation throughout your organization, management must:

- Spell out expectations regarding innovative behavior.

- Publicize and promote the kind of behavior you seek.

- Create a curriculum of innovation.

- Provide basic training in creativity.

- Provide more advanced innovation training to select groups.

Spelling Out Expectations   It's truly amazing what can happen when employees are inveighed to "be innovative" as part of daily work. The challenge to leadership is to continually find new ways to spur employees at every level and in every part of the organization to think boldly and creatively about what such thinking might produce. It's the role of leadership to push people to see beyond their narrow job functions.

The notion of institutionalizing innovation is new. Involving rank and file employees in the process is downright radical. But so was Total Quality Management when it first appeared on the scene, and now we take its precepts for granted. Slowly but surely, companies are beginning to look for a new set of competencies and behaviors from their people. Competence in one's specialty, whether finance or logistics or purchasing, is no longer enough.

Until only recently, specialist thinking has dominated organizations. "A lot of times the best marketing ideas don't come from marketing," notes Jon Letzler, division president of Atlanta-based apparel maker Russell Athletic. "I came up through marketing and my experience has been that marketing people think they own the interface with the customer."

Letzler might have added that the finance people think they have a monopoly on finance, logistics on logistics, etc. This "silo thinking" has permeated organizational thinking since Frederick Taylor taught the world that specialization equated with efficiency. To a point, Taylor was right, but efficiency and innovation are different kettles of fish.

To respond effectively to turbulent external forces, companies need employees capable of generating ideas that don't come from their specialty cookbooks. The competencies and behaviors that are becoming most important for firms to nurture and reward center around the creative process: how to come up with novel ideas, that, when implemented, become novel solutions.

Publicizing Innovative Behavior   When that 12-person team in the logistics department comes up with an idea that increases safety, that's news you want to spread. Leaders of innovation get the word out. When your sales rep in Seattle spots a new type of packaging and is instrumental in getting an 18-month exclusive license that puts you out in front of competitors, that's innovation.

Obviously, people deep within the organization who seldom if ever come in contact with a real live customer are more apt to come up with process ideas. Sales, marketing, and customer service people are more apt to come up with product or business model ideas, but not always.

Creating a Curriculum of Innovation   Because innovation is such a new field, in most organizations today there's still a great deal of what might be called "innovation illiteracy." Employees and managers alike simply don't understand enough about the way the organization works, the needs of customers, what its goals are, and what the numbers mean, to know how to meaningfully contribute to the company's strategic success.

Moreover, how can employees and managers make appropriate and useful suggestions for improvement *of the innovation process* if they don't know the difference between a process improvement and a strategy idea? How can employees know whether to suggest that a new venture team do X, if they can't easily find out? How can employees have profit-producing ideas when they don't know how profit is measured?

Company leaders often assume that rank and file employees can't understand financial information. Yet, after even cursory exposure to the numbers, companies that have offered training almost universally find that employees of all backgrounds and educational levels can learn, are interested in learning, and are in a much better position to contribute. Knowledge of the company's financial and growth objectives makes employees feel that their work—and their ideas—are part of a larger whole. By showing employees where and how they can impact the numbers, they get ideas on how they can personally contribute.

Basic Training in Creativity   When basic training in creativity, problem solving, and the steps in the innovation process are part of an overall strategy that has the support of senior management, employee creativity begins to open up. They realize not only that ideas are important, but that *their* ideas are important. They also begin to see that as with most things in life, "if it's gonna be, it's up to me." It's one thing to have an idea and want to submit it to a suggestion system or a supervisor or somebody else who will run with it. Without training, that's where they want to believe it ends. "I've come up with this idea and I gave it to my manager, done."

But it isn't done. The problem is that there is neither time nor motivation on the part of the organization to act on other people's ideas. Their manager is probably just as overworked and busy as they are. That's why teaching the basics of innovation literacy gives people the tools and the training to sort through their own ideas and better gauge the potential of the idea before going further. Then, if it meets the criteria, they themselves can champion the idea more effectively, and if it's a simple idea affecting their own work, they are empowered to simply go ahead and do it.

More Advanced Innovation Training for Select Groups   After teaching the building blocks of innovation, select employees must be introduced to new approaches to driving growth through innovation. Pursuing new markets, the latest customer listening techniques, idea management, strategies, rapid prototyping, and new venture incubating as practiced by leading firms should be taught. The purpose of such programs is more than the sum of their parts. Employees become entrepreneurs. They think like real world entrepreneurs for the company's future.

Quite a large number of organizations teach problem-solving techniques, while others teach creativity. These courses are generally heavy on ideation and creativity, but gloss over what we'll call the "business case," in other words, how an idea will contribute to the company's objectives. Result: Most employees and even managers don't have a clue as to how to make their ideas happen.

Training for your most promising employees must center on the innovation process: how to take ideas, develop them, and move them to the goal line of implementation. This requires marshaling resources, networking, building the buy-in, and so forth. To do these things—the creative coupled with the innovative—requires that leadership be dispersed as widely as possible, as this kind of activity is impossible to dictate from above.

Leadership Strategy 3:
Allocate Resources and Decide on Levels of Risk

Organizations have three essential resources to allocate: time, money, and talent. And no matter how progressive the system, allocating resources is, at root, a leadership function. You are either going to spend $8 million to build that prototype to test the market's receptivity, or you are not. You are either going to pull key people away from regular line functions to be part of a cross-functional team that will work on the new strategy innovation, or you are not.

Innovation-adept companies aren't roll-of-the-dice risk-takers, they're risk-managers. Because they go about opportunity invention in a systematic, organized fashion, they don't "shoot from the hip" or act "on the chairman's whim." And while they suffer losses and go down unproductive boulevards in pursuit of growth, their losses are not catastrophic.

Such firms recognize that their risk-managers are not the enemy, but rather that they play a vital role in understanding the true extent of the firm's possible exposure, rather than allowing for unpleasant surprises later. Risks are dealt with at various decision points in the stages of each idea's development. If the idea is for a currently served market and is not radical in nature, it can be developed and analyzed in stages through a process many companies now rigorously adhere to and that will be covered in Chapter 7: "Producing Powerful Products."

While leaders must ultimately be the ones to allocate resources, in Innovation Vanguard companies, a process is in place that rationalizes the task of deciding which ideas to fund, which people to involve, and how much time will need to be devoted. The CEO's role becomes not so much the venture-capitalist-in-chief as an orchestrator of the overall process.

Leadership Strategy 4:
Establish Innovation Metrics

Look around your organization and chances are you'll find dozens of measuring systems in place: ROI, net earnings, growth, IBIT, EVA—it's quite a list. These yardsticks all measure past performance not future potential. They are lagging indicators, whereas innovation metrics are leading indicators. Other systems measure efficiency, cost reduction, market share of existing products and services, etc. And of course, individuals and groups are measured via performance reviews that may or may not include yardsticks of innovative results.

There's no question that measuring anything is tricky, and measuring "innovation" is even trickier. So tricky in fact that some seasoned executives who are pro-innovation maintain that measuring business growth and profitability are good enough indicators of a company's efforts in this regard, and that measuring innovation can backfire, giving you "innovation for innovation's sake."

For most firms, however, establishing new metrics will be essential. Without them, you don't have a clue as to how well you are doing. Executives in the Innovation Vanguard companies agree that the way you measure innovation progress (or lack thereof) determines the type of innovation you get, and the degree of magnitude as well. If a manager, team or department is being measured (and rewarded) on short-term objectives for example, the vision will likely be short term as well. This can cause longer-term ideas to be relegated to the back burner permanently. Metrics tend to determine whether your company's focus will be on incremental innovation or on breakthroughs; on products or processes or business model changes.

Here are some guidelines on metrics:

1. Measure percent of revenue from new products and services.

2. Avoid creating disunity.

3. Measure your pipeline.

Measure Percent of Revenue from New Products and Services   The most popular form of measuring innovation progress is to plot percentage of this year's sales revenues that come from products/services introduced in the past (generally four or five) years. In recent years, leading firms have often boasted in their annual reports about the high percentage of revenue derived from products introduced during the past four or five years. 3M, which makes products ranging from Scotch Tape to asthmatic inhalers and liquid crystal display screens, along with 50,000 other items, has long maintained a policy that each division create 25 percent of its sales from products introduced within the past five years.

The evidence for doing so is based on solid research. "The proportion of new products and services is a key indicator of corporate success (a correlative link, not directly causal) both in terms of revenue enhancement and total shareholder returns," concludes the PricewaterhouseCooper study of 399 global companies we reported on in Chapter 1. What the PWC data clearly suggests is that if a company makes it a goal to increase the proportion of turnover from new products and services, then, over time, that firm is likely to benefit from a higher growth rate than competitors that do not.

Avoid Creating Disunity   In 1992, 3M's new CEO Livio DeSimone raised the products metric even higher. He decreed that *30 percent* of sales were to come from products less than four years old. But do such decrees and measurements actually lead to increased turnover? Or do they create more look-alike products, line extensions, and micro-improvements that satisfy quotas but don't turbocharge growth?

Certain innovation researchers quote an unidentified 3M senior executive who told them that when managers needed to meet DeSimone's the new products quota, they would often do the equivalent of simply changing the color of the product from red to green. The policy "put so much pressure on research and development to turn out new products that the research labs had a natural reluctance to devote time to improving older products." In 1996, according to these researchers, "3M began to quietly downplay this policy."

Did they really? Since 3M is an Innovation Vanguard firm, we wanted to find out more. A spokesperson told us the company still holds to the 30 percent new in the four-year yardstick. "We do measure replacement products [as opposed to entirely new products]," she observed, "and we want replacement products to be less than half these new products." As far as downplaying the policy, not true, according to her sources.

"We also aim at changing the mix of our new products with more emphasis on products truly new to the world, instead of line extensions. When we began this effort, two out of three new product sales dollars came from replacements. Today, the opposite is true; completely new products are producing two out of three sales dollars."

By a completely new product, 3M means something on the order of Post-it Notes; it is original to the marketplace. By line extension, 3M means new forms of Post-it products, such as new designs and formats, different colors, and additional sizes.

While 3M refined its metrics to create alignment around the need for breakthrough as well as incremental and substantial innovation, some companies strive to develop a portfolio of new product types and degrees. This helps diversify risk and provides a balanced investment approach to innovation.

For companies just setting out to establish innovation metrics, the key measure of success is not just avoiding disunity, but motivating behavior change on the part of key business unit leaders such that they make innovation a priority. Again, 3M's pioneering experience at least for manufacturing sector firms, indicates how complex it is to encourage innovation.

Here's how Paul Guehler, 3M's senior vice president of research and development, describes the issue: "Let's say you pay on division profit sharing, and [unit executives'] year end bonuses are based strictly on profit growth. Well, they are not going to do anything to develop new products, because they don't want to take a hit on profits, so that doesn't work. But if you reward strictly on sales growth, then the tendency is to forgo profits and drive growth in an unprofitable manner. So you have to have a balance in your formula that rewards growth and profits, and you've also got to factor in new businesses into the equation, and you also have to be able to fund entire new businesses from existing profits."

Clearly, as Guehler's many years of experience indicate, designing metrics that motivate and don't have untoward consequences is a key responsibility of leadership and needs to be well thought-out and deemed to be fair and clear, lest it become a problem later.

Measure Your Pipeline   Measuring product turnover is essential but is still rear-view mirror measuring. The vast majority of organizations today measure existing and past business activity, not future business activity, such as the number of new and promising ideas in your new product pipeline.

PWC's research indicates that successful product innovators are also those who are most able to innovate more broadly across processes and business models. Yet the study also found that few of the companies studied had mechanisms for relating their output measures back to the internal drivers of those measures (such as launch rates, success rates, time-to-market rates). The highest performers in the survey use a balanced scorecard to measure their innovation performance, both in terms of outcomes and also in terms of the processes that led to those outcomes. The report concluded that: "Innovation is complex and dynamic and measurement systems need to reflect this."

Leadership Strategy 5:
Reward Innovation

The question any manager or individual contributor asked to innovate immediately asks is, why? Why should I try to put forth a new idea? Why should I volunteer to be part of this special team when I am already overwhelmed with work? And why, when "failure" could adversely affect my career?

Your innovation strategy should address these issues squarely, which inevitably means thinking through how you will reward and encourage innovation.

Whatever you come up with as rewards, remember this: The rewards for risk-taking must always outweigh the fallout from failure. Rewarding innovation specifically sits within a wider context of how other behaviors are rewarded.

What you reward is what you get, the old saying has it. With innovation, it's really no different. Reward compliance and conformity and you get compliance and conformity. Reward execution (flawlessly achieving short-term objectives), and you'll get that. Reward optimization versus pioneering and that's what you'll get.

Here are two guidelines for rewarding innovative behavior:

1. Reward innovative behavior intrinsically and extrinsically.

2. Reward through recognition.

Reward Intrinsically and Extrinsically   Million-dollar ideas from individual contributors not on a bonus plan should be rewarded financially. But beyond this deserved extrinsic reward is the intrinsic one—expressing our innate desire to create and to improve our circumstances. In innovation circles, it is a widely accepted notion that what motivates people to want to "bring new ideas to life" are not extrinsic rewards (those coming from the outside) but intrinsic (coming from inside ourselves). It's often illustrated with a story that we fear will strike you as mean-spirited.

An old man lived near an elementary school, and every day after school some kids would stand on his lawn and shout epithets at him: "You stupid old geezer; you wrinkly old prune"—and worse. The man came up with a plan. One day he walked out while the kids were screaming at him and said, "If you kids come back here tomorrow, I'll give each of you a dollar."

Now this was a surprise, and they came back even earlier the next day, and showed even more enthusiasm in their name-calling. As promised, the old man again paid his tormentors and said, "If you come back tomorrow, I'll pay each of you a quarter." The kids still thought that was a pretty good deal, so they showed up the next day and let him have it again. Then he said, "If you come back tomorrow, I'll give each of you a penny." The kids could hardly believe their ears. "A penny?" they said. "Forget it." And they never came back again.

This classic story has a lot to say about rewarding innovation because it addresses the issue of why people do what they do. What in fact constitutes a reward? Commonly we think of money, recognition, stock options, the usual things. But what is often overlooked or misunderstood entirely is that people want to create. Simply being invited to be a player in a new project is a reward in itself.

Reward Through Recognition   When it comes to rewarding innovation behavior, leaders have a lot more ways of doing so available to them than many realize. Simply showing enthusiasm when someone brings up an idea and offers to "look into it further" is a type of reward in itself. When a senior person or company publicly lauds the accomplishments of an individual or team, this is a "reward" of sorts. Such a visit had a lifelong impact on 3M researcher Roger Appledorn. The president of the company dropped by the newly hired scientist's laboratory one morning. Appledorn, years later, could still recall what the man said to him: "Son, I hear you're doing something interesting, tell me about it." That visit kept motivating Roger for nearly four decades, and even more importantly, it taught him how to motivate others.

Listening and showing interest is a big part of the job of encouraging innovation. It's amazing how the little things can be huge when it comes to encouraging the type of behavior we're after. One simple way is to visit with the people in the organization in their offices to talk about their work, their progress, their ideas, their passion.

Designing Your 21st Century Approach to Leadership

No system to encourage and foster innovation is perfect. But by wrestling with the issues and questions this chapter raises, you'll be far along in designing a process that is right for your firm. Leadership is critical to innovation, and leading innovation requires new approaches, some of which delegate responsibility for making it happen and some that leaders cannot delegate.

Innovation requires one additional thing: a conducive culture. And that is a subject we take up in the next chapter.

CHAPTER 3

Creating the Culture

I don't want any "yes men" in this organization.
I want people to speak their minds, even if it does cost them their jobs.
—Sam Goldwyn

Changing a company's culture is never easy. Yet the good news, based on our study of Innovation Vanguard companies, is that with the right leadership, cultures *can* be reshaped and amazing results can accrue. This chapter will provide you with the key factors to focus on and approaches you can use to develop a comprehensive strategy to align your culture with your innovation objectives. Let's start with a much-needed definition.

What Is Culture, Anyway?

Culture refers to an organization's values, beliefs, and behaviors. It is transmitted through subtle cues, through employees sharing their interpretations of events, and largely through the behaviors and attitudes of leaders that signal what is expected.

If an organization values "playing it safe," risk-taking is inherently discouraged. If it values cohesion, loyalty to the company way, conformity, and blind obedience to authority, then it devalues their opposites. If it hires people that comfortably "go along to get along," then it devalues those who are inclined to challenge rules and boundaries. If a culture is "cutthroat, competitive, and secretive," as the once high-flying Enron has been described after its collapse, it cannot be also humane, collegial, or open as well.

A company's culture may or may not be conducive to promoting innovation. Its reward system may be at odds with encouraging people to want to try something that may not work. Its hiring practices may weed out maverick personality types.

It's easy for leaders to say to employees, "We want you to take risks, we want creative ideas bubbling forth, we want you to think outside that box, oh, and we also want you to make your numbers, and we don't want failure." The message that gets translated to the farther reaches of the organization: Make your numbers and we don't want failure.

Culture is often revealed in the stories employees tell each other. At firms with a long history of innovation, the stories remind people that it is safe to take risks. Robert Johnson, one of the founders of Johnson & Johnson, congratulated a manager who lost money on a failed new product by telling him, "Son, if you're making mistakes, that means you are making decisions and taking risks." Similarly, the oral history at 3M revolves around tales of the early days when the company introduced one product failure after another before it began to succeed wildly. At Disney, many employees are aware that the idea of opening Disney stores was suggested by a rank and file employee.

Fear—The Enemy of an Innovative Culture

Fear is the most prevalent enforcer of a company's cultural norms. People fear failure, ridicule, loss of face, loss of legitimacy, loss of one's job. Fear of being sent to Siberia. Mary Jean Ryan, president and CEO of SSM Health Care System in St. Louis observes that fear has been the "standard operating procedure" in healthcare organizations for years.

In that culture, according to Ryan, a budding administrator's professional growth would be signaled by increased mastery of military style command and control. "I recall an instructor whose way of checking to see whether management trainees were doing a good job in their supervisory roles was to ask them to identify someone they had recently fired or disciplined," Ryan wrote in *Healthcare Forum Journal.* Hiring the "right" people, monitoring them closely, and firing them when they failed to be commanded and controlled were the manager's primary tasks.

Although Ryan was describing healthcare organizations, she could just as easily have been describing organizations in other industries. Fear is the enemy of an innovative culture because it tends to arrest the very activities necessary for it to take place. All of that was well and good during a period of stability. But healthcare, like many other industries, is no longer stable but has become super-competitive, knowledge-intensive, and fast-changing.

From Controlling Behavior to Shaping Behavior

To respond to these new conditions, SSM Health Care, under Ryan's leadership, realized it needed new ideas to come from all corners of the organization, not just from the top. In the old culture observed Ryan, "there was not much encouragement to innovate and create, to listen to those who were not as 'high up' in the hierarchy, or to look proactively at all levels of the organization for ways to improve the products and services being offered." Like EDS and many other companies, SSM Health Care needed to create an innovation-adept culture. But how?

Suddenly asking for innovative behavior from employees may not only confuse but is unlikely to stimulate major changes in perspective needed to produce results. Efforts to improve innovation on a short-term crash basis, or in a select part of the organization, have little or no effect on the enterprise *because they go against the prevailing cultural norms.*

University of California psychology professor Charlan Nemeth examined companies that were identified as being "built to last," meaning that they had been successful over a long period of time. From the standpoint of their cultures being conducive to innovation, Nemeth issued this warning: "The very cultural traits that made these companies successful may in fact preclude their ability to invent radically different futures." Nemeth looks for the clues to a company's culture in subtle on-the-job socialization in "how we do things at this company," meaning the correct, accepted way. Sometimes it is made clear in the form of approval or disapproval by peers and continual ranking and performance appraisals that separate the good guys from the bad, and increasingly, none too subtly asks the "bottom tier" to leave the company.

While such cultures are highly productive and efficient, they tend to "eject like a virus" those who do not fit the mold. Yet these very nonconforming qualities are key to innovative thinking, Nemeth observes. To conceive and introduce the truly new, you and your people must be unhindered by these forces. You must feel free to "deviate" from "the way we've always done it around here," to question big and little assumptions, paradigms, conventional wisdom, thinking styles, and other received ways of viewing things.

Creating the Culture: What Doesn't Work

Based on recent studies, we now have clear guidelines as to what doesn't work in creating a more adept culture.

Take the innovation center for example. Millions of dollars have been spent to set up and fund these centers with the specific charter of stimulating new business and product ideas. "But after 10–15 years of these programs, most have been terminated. Most of the individuals [who were appointed to run them] have left the companies," notes a study conducted by the Association of Managers for Innovation, an informal group of 50 current and former innovation center leaders for Fortune 500 firms. They have been meeting for over 20 years to discuss experiences and technology related to the area of organizational innovation.

The approaches of these company-sponsored centers differed widely. Some were independent funding sources, while others were simple facilitation and encouragement staffs. Others provided creativity-ideation rooms. Most made an effort to make the center distinct from normal business activities, and often, the funding came from individual business units. Sometimes these programs were combined informally with an acquisition or venture capital effort. Almost all of the centers' efforts were centralized within the R&D function.

All of these efforts succeeded in generating new ideas, sometimes generating significant new businesses. Indeed, according to Jack Hipple, who led the study, "many new products currently in the marketplace can be identified, many years later, with these programs." So why were they disbanded?

"The biggest barrier to success in these programs was their nearly exclusive focus on the research and development function," concludes Hipple. "In many cases, these programs were funded at the expense of existing business technology budgets and had virtually no involvement of the commercial or marketing arms of the corporations." This type of sponsorship, over time, opened the door to "subtle forms of sabotage by the business units" looking to meet short-term objectives and take care of current customers. In addition, "the costs and impact of these programs were not clearly thought out ahead of time in a way that could be communicated clearly to senior management." Further, sponsorship was too narrow to have staying power, meaning that such programs sometimes withered "because of the retirement of just one key person." And, lastly, the time horizons for top- and bottom-line impact were usually seriously underestimated.

Thus, these programs proved these two concepts:

- A centralized creativity center cannot significantly impact the bottom line of an organization.

- The R&D function, alone, cannot significantly affect an organization's long-term bottom line or new business development.

Clearly, it is time to rethink innovation, and to look for methods that do work to drive revenue momentum. In this regard, we can learn from our survey of Innovation Vanguard companies the elements necessary for long-term success.

The Post-it Story

Creating an innovation-adept culture has a lot to do with how "innovative activity" is viewed by people in the organization: how it is looked upon by management, the emphasis it is given, the resources that are devoted to it, the types of people who work in the company, and how successfully the barriers that inhibit it from happening are dealt with and overcome.

In Chapter 1 we observed that innovation, in its simplest definition, is "coming up with ideas and bringing them to life." Think about your favorite example of a breakthrough product, service, or business model. Now consider all the things that had to happen from "aha" to "bringing it to life." Take the Post-it Note, for example. The story goes that Art Fry came up with the idea while singing in the choir at St. Paul Presbyterian Church.

Fry had a problem: The little scraps of paper he used to mark pages in his hymnal kept falling out, and he was having trouble keeping up. A solution occurred to him, involving a sticky substance that a colleague at work had invented, but hadn't been able to find a use for. The glue had unusual properties: It would stick fairly well, and it would allow you to unstick it as well. Aha, thought Fry, maybe this could be a new product for 3M, little sticky notes that people could use for various things.

All well and good, Art Fry had fulfilled the first part of innovation: he'd come up with the idea. The story of the second half of the definition, "bringing it to life," is much longer, so we'll summarize.

Fry experimented with the glue and little pieces of paper, got others in his department enthused about his idea (especially the chap who'd come up with the glue), and continued to develop the idea. He even got funding to spend money to develop the idea and overcame skepticism from peers who doubted if consumers would pay for tiny pieces of paper when they could simply use scratch paper. Well, finally the product was officially launched to a resoundingly indifferent market.

As Fry himself explained, the "bringing to life" portion of innovation was, for his idea, anything but straightforward, even in a company known for its culture of innovation. "We had a difficult time building the buy-in for Post-it Notes," Fry told *Fast Company* magazine. "People in 3M just couldn't see that there was a big enough market. Stores were reluctant to stock the new product. Customers didn't know how to use them."

The story goes that the original product sold so poorly that senior management wanted to scrap it. In desperation, Fry and his team loaded up suitcases of Post-it Notes and headed for Boise, Idaho, where they handed out samples of the product to passersby in an attempt to get people to reorder. They sent samples to corporate administrative assistants hoping that, once they used the new product, they also would want to reorder. Needless to say, the product caught on from there.

Post-it Notes now add billions of dollars to 3M's overall revenues each year. It also gives us a window into the multifaceted, multidimensional process that is innovation. While inventing the future is often exciting and even exhilarating at times ("the most fun I have ever had with my clothes on," someone once termed it), it's also one of the more complex forms of human endeavor.

If you were to use time-lapse photography to film the "making of an idea" from vision to successful product, what you would see would be a series of discrete activities that must be performed by a team—make that an entire company—of people. Think about the skills that are needed along the way to accomplish this development. Opportunity-sensing and idea-hatching, or else Fry would never even have hatched the idea. And then, a panoply of problem-solving and the meshing of specialized skills of teams of people who turned that idea into a breakthrough product.

The process, if we unpack it, involves tons of experimentation, developing and applying technologies to design and develop the new offering, prototyping, piloting, costing, and tons of reworking, refining, rethinking, and learning. And "failing" as well. Look at all the experimentation that had to take place—even after launch.

Well, innovation in your firm probably doesn't involve launching the next Post-it Note. But here's the point: The rate at which you and people in your company come up with promising ideas, do feasibility research, obtain funding, build prototypes, gather feedback from potential users, pilot launch, solve problems, improvise solutions, and overcome hurdles and barriers is the rate at which innovation occurs. Or doesn't occur. And culture is at the heart and soul of every one of these activities, either serving to catalyze innovative behavior—or thwart it.

Creating an Innovation-Adept Culture

The box on page 65 lists eleven strategies designed to guide you in improving your firm's culture for greater innovation effectiveness. Let's look at each topic in detail.

Culture Strategy 1:
Assess Variance Between Present Climate and Optimum Climate

Assessing this is not as difficult as it may sound. In fact, when I'm conducting a kickoff seminar for a company wanting to seriously look at its innovation process with an eye toward improvement, I actually perform such an assessment with what is usually the management team in real time. I simply ask participants to rate on a scale of 1 to 10 (with 10 being highly innovative and 1 being innovation-challenged in the extreme) the present climate for innovation in their company. After those votes are passed to my assistant to begin finding the average number, I ask participants to rate what they believe to be the "optimal climate" for innovation, given competitive challenges, growth goals, and so forth. After these votes are also tallied and an aggregate number tabulated, I'll ask the group for their thoughts. Having done this exercise with a wide variety of companies in the United States and other countries, I then show these managers what is usually a significant gap in their present culture and their ideal or optimal culture.

Although you may not have the ability to poll your management team just now for their perceptions on these two questions "where are we now?" versus "where do we need to be to meet the growth challenge?" you do have your own perceptions to go on regarding where your company presently resides culturally. Based on numerous surveys of this sort with clients, I find that most companies rate themselves and their present climate at or below average, while they see that to accomplish their growth goals, they must optimally become an 8 or 9.

How do you get there? That leads us to topic 2.

Culture Strategy 2:
Describe Barriers to Innovation

Consider all impediments to accelerated "idea to profits" activity in all spheres of your firm, both structurally and culturally. By structurally, we mean things like "lack of an innovation process" such that people know what to do with their ideas once they hatch them. Structurally also could mean that your firm lacks a funding mechanism for ideas that don't fall neatly into the purview of an existing business unit, or that are more radical and longer term. Cultural barriers would be perceived punishment for "failure," a culture that

**Improving Your Firm's Culture for
Greater Innovation Effectiveness**

1. Assess the variance between the firm's present climate for innovation and the optimum climate.

2. Describe your organization's barriers to innovation.

3. Describe your current innovation process.

4. Address the "lack of time" barrier.

5. Put practices in place that cause openness.

6. Balance the mix of people to ensure a conducive culture.

7. Identify mavericks in your company.

8. Improve the system or change the system.

9. Examine your attitude regarding innovation and individual contribution.

10. Identify and develop champions.

11. Identify and recruit innovators.

prizes conformity, loyalty to management that really means obedience to authority, lack of risk-taking as a result of such conformity, and so forth.

It's worth it to do this analysis right, which means either developing a survey instrument yourself, as Citigroup did, or using one that already exists. Various consultants in the field of innovation, as well as a number of global consulting firms, have devised a variety of assessment tools and benchmarking surveys that can give you an unbiased assessment of your firm's cultural climate for innovation.

A quick way to focus on possible barriers to innovation is to ask yourself some questions: What happens to creative people in your organization? What happens when someone fails? What stories are told by people in your company about the perils and/or rewards for risk-taking? What type of behavior vis-à-vis innovation does senior management really want? Does management really walk the talk? Such questions get at the heart of your company's cultural climate for innovation.

Culture Strategy 3:
Describe Your Current Innovation Process

If you're slightly or completely stumped by this, don't worry, you're not alone. By far, it's the most frequent barrier to innovation. "People don't know what to do with their ideas and don't know how to take action on them." According to one innovation best practices survey, fewer than one in three companies use a formal process to collect ideas. An equally small number have an ideation or innovation committee for collecting, screening, and taking action on growth-producing ideas and improvements.

By contrast, all of the Innovation Vanguard companies studied for this book have comprehensive "idea management" systems in place that assist them in approaching innovation in a fundamentally different way.

These systems come in quite a few varieties and aren't mutually exclusive (many companies researched for this book have more than one program in place). We'll examine the different systems in greater depth in Chapter 4, but for now, it's important from the standpoint of improving a company's culture to note that single-handedly, these systems overcome the biggest impediment to enterprise-wide innovation, which is: lack of a process.

Culture Strategy 4:
Address the "Lack of Time" Barrier

If you're like most knowledge workers today, you're putting in a lot of hours on the job. About 163 hours more each year (an extra month a year, in essence) than a similar person in the workforce 30 years ago. Clearly, the "doing more with less" trend really means in most companies "doing more with fewer people."

The increasingly frazzled, multitasking, constantly interrupted work style is a real innovation inhibitor. Each day, according to a recent study, knowledge workers receive 52 phone interruptions, 36 e-mails, 23 voicemails, in addition to a barrage of other intrusions, electronic and otherwise. The result: workers who are over-connected, overcommitted, overworked, and overwhelmed.

Is it any wonder that, after "no innovation process" the next most common barrier is "lack of time to innovate." Lack of time inhibits innovation by crowding out reflection time that can produce fresh approaches of accomplishing particular goals or dreaming up the company's next breakthrough. In this technology-induced "always on" atmosphere, if somebody is seen quietly sitting at his or her desk thinking, that person may be perceived to be loafing.

Companies can more easily make demands on their employees from afar, simply by providing them with the latest techno-gadgets. In an attempt to be more productive, companies outfit their troops with devices that make them reachable anywhere, at any hour. Forty-one percent of employers supply at least some of their workers with cell phones or pagers, while 57 percent provide laptop computers for off-premise use, notes one survey. The ability to escape the day-to-day pressures and deadlines becomes impossible. Lack of time diminishes the desire to advocate for, much less follow through on, bold new ideas.

Recent attempts to deal with the issue include:

- Every other Friday at S.C. Johnson & Sons, a placard is posted on the door of all conference rooms: "Room Sealed by Order of 'No Meeting Day' Police." Twice a month, the Racine, Wisconsin maker of Windex, Pledge wax, Ziploc storage bags, and other household products, bans meetings by its 3500 U.S. employees.

- Microsoft offers senior executives as much work-free time off as they need—in addition to annual vacations of up to five weeks and a sabbatical every seven years.

- Intel workshops encourage time-stretched workers to tell supervisors to stop calling them at home at night. Otherwise, "we're always on, like electronic service men always on call," laments an Intel technology-education manager.

- Southwest Airlines organizes a monthly "Thinking Day."

Such attempts to address the time barrier are a start—they show that firms are aware of this barrier to innovation. But few companies, even among the most progressive, are willing to take more dramatic steps to include an allocation of time in their overall innovation strategy.

One of the few companies to have addressed the time inhibitor is 3M, which gives all its employees 15 percent of their time to pursue their own ideas. It turns out that even at this bellwether company, the forces of efficiency have led to the downplaying of this oft-cited practice. Research and Development chief Paul Guehler told us that the 15 percent free-time concept "is not a written rule, I view it as we have eighty-five percent managed time." That's no doubt news to the many companies that have attempted to emulate 3M, such as Corning, whose 10 percent free-time policy, at least for scientists, has led to numerous "Friday afternoon projects" that have paid off.

The question at the heart of ameliorating this barrier is, if people are given more time, would there necessarily be more innovation? Would there be a greater tendency to discover and implement better processes, products, and services? Or would the tendency be to simply expand the remaining workload to fill the available time?

To be sure, an abundance of time does not guarantee more creative output, just as a lack of time doesn't always mean less innovativeness. The issue is not that simple. Employees and managers may list "lack of time" as a barrier to innovation, but hiring more people and cutting people's workload won't necessarily lead to more of it.

Indeed, innovators often point to a time crunch to meet a deadline that led them to stop ignoring a problem and come up with a novel solution. Often it is during "crunch times" that employees see the inadequacies of the firm's present processes, methods, and safeguards. Similarly, it is during times of stress that customers reveal the limitations of your company's products or services, such as your ability to customize or not customize, or your ability to deliver more quickly than normal.

The sales rep in the field office sees that "there's got to be a better way" of processing her order and comes up with an idea to do just that. The team busily preparing for the all-important exhibit at the industry trade show comes up with ideas that dramatically improve next year's process. The consulting team busy preparing a bid proposal by the promised date is spurred to redesign its system so that next time won't require an all-nighter. All of these are examples of how innovativeness can turn "lack of time" from being a barrier to being a booster. Necessity is the mother of innovation.

It's only when people are required to work at such a pace all the time that "lack of time" becomes the mother of all barriers. When a company is doing well, looking to explain its uncommon success, it often notes with pride that the leader "drives his people hard" and has an "incredible work ethic." One such leader, chairman of a national retail chain, was invariably lauded for working his people at a frenetic pace throughout a decade. But then the company began to lose its edge and missed trends, its stores fell behind the times, growth stalled, and its stock price tanked. Key talent departed in droves. Tired of the 60–70 hour weeks, a cultural trait that had been viewed as a plus had become a burden.

Clearly, when "lack of time" surfaces on internal surveys as a perceived barrier to innovation, you must delve deeply into the issue. Are people trying to send a message to senior management? Is there a deeper problem? Is "lack of time" symptomatic of deeper anxieties and frustrations? Will granting free time to work on innovation have the desired effect? It's not a simple barrier to ameliorate, but correct understanding is critical.

Culture Strategy 5:
Institute Practices that Create Openness

Companies with a high awareness of culture's importance to innovation have visible, tangible, and frequently humorous reminders that it's okay to take risks—that a person won't be beheaded for sincere attempts that fail.

Hewlett-Packard engineer Chuck House became something of a legend when he defied cofounder David Packard and continued surreptitious development of a computer graphics project that he believed in. Ultimately the product was a big moneymaker for H-P, and a Chuck House Medal of Defiance was created honoring his persistence. Esso Resources of Canada presents the Royal Order of the Duck, a wooden duck's head mounted on a toilet plunger. This object sits on the desk of the person who sticks his or her neck out and does something without approval.

At Medtronic, a program called Quest awards up to $50,000 to pursue "proof of concept" of ideas that R&D management has rejected. "Sometimes the ideas compete with something the company is already doing and would not get funding within the normal structure of things for a variety of reasons," explains Dr. Glen Nelson, Medtronic's innovation czar and vice chairman. "Whether it's too far out or whether it's counterintuitive, the whole idea of funding these ideas is to make sure that we allow the devil's advocates to prove something will work when [management] doesn't think it will."

Each year half a dozen Quest projects get funded and a number of them over the years have become real products. One such product is Reveal, a small implantable EKG loop recorder. "Everyone said it wouldn't work, even the customers," recalls Nelson. "I can tell you if you have an individual with a real belief and you give him enough time to prove it, he'll prove everyone wrong including the customers. If we hadn't funded a skunkworks for Reveal, I don't think that idea would have ever reached the market."

Culture Strategy 6:
Balance the Mix of People

Diversity is a word oft-used these days to describe variance in gender, age, ethnicity, and country of origin. Certainly this type of diversity is helpful in creative thinking. But diversity of thinking styles and the ability to see things differently is another kind of diversity that is less understood. Nevertheless, we can agree that it will be highly useful and valued in the 21st century.

Most companies are concerned with attracting and retaining "talented" people. By this they mean intelligent, experienced "team players." But such "talented" people are different from the kind of people you need to ignite and sustain innovation. The essential mix for teams, work groups, business units, and even entire companies really means balancing three different personality types: mavericks, individual contributors (Culture Stategy 9, on page 74), and champions (Culture Strategy 10, on page 75).

Culture Strategy 7:
Identify Mavericks

Pat Farrah has been called wacko and a genius depending on whom you talk to. However, people at Home Depot agree on one thing: He's a maverick. After helping found the Atlanta–based home improvement chain in the late 1970s with Bernard Marcus and Arthur Blank, Farrah burned out and left the firm to pursue other interests.

Returning a decade later, he was soon up to his nonconformist antics. When a store manager made excuses about slow progress on a store renovation, Farrah hopped on a forklift and knocked down an interior wall that needed to be removed. He has been known to take a chain saw in hand to demolish product displays that he deemed insufficiently alluring.

"Just a wild man," in the words of one former Home Depot executive. "Known for his crazy ideas," chimes in another, describing how Farrah once priced fireplace screens at one store at a quarter of the price of a nearby rival. Veterans further recall the time Home Depot was opening a store in Florida and Farrah snatched catalogs from a rival chain and hung them in the new Home Depot outlet with signs promising prices 20 percent lower.

Often called mavericks, or cowboys or free thinkers, folks like Pat Farrah are cut from a different cloth. They don't thrive on blending in, or "going along to get along" or being popular. They really don't know how. Sometimes they seem incapable of doing anything but causing trouble. They are the kind of individuals who look at things differently because they themselves are different. They would rather ask for forgiveness than for permission. They are not big on "social skills."

Do you have at least a few such people in your company? You'd better. You need them! They are essential to a climate conducive to creativity. The Pat Farrahs of this world help keep complacency at bay, they ask those "have you thought about" or "what if" questions that nobody else thinks of or is willing to ask. They are the individuals who, in highly regimented environments, have all been sent packing, if they somehow managed to get hired in the first place.

When they get interested in something, these folks bore into it deeply. They are excited by the thrill of the hunt—whether it be for information or for novel solutions to vexing problems. These are the people most likely to come up with the ideas that become tomorrow's breakthroughs.

If this personality type seems fuzzy, the role mavericks play in fostering innovation is anything but. Social scientists' studies such as those conducted by University of California Berkeley's Charlan Nemeth confirm time and again that we humans tend to be a conforming-prone race. "When people are faced with a majority of others who agree on a particular attitude or judgment, they are very likely to adopt the majority judgment," says Nemeth. "Even when using objective issues, such as judging the length of lines, people will ignore the information from their own senses and adopt an erroneous majority view."

The question is: Why? "The available evidence suggests that there are two primary reasons for adopting normative or majority views, even when incorrect," suggests Nemeth. "One is that people assume that truth lies in numbers and are quick to infer that they themselves are incorrect when faced with a unanimous majority. The other reason is that they fear disapproval and rejection for being different." Most of us loathe suggesting an idea for fear of ridicule and rejection. Mavericks, like antibodies, keep the organization healthy and safe.

For years, in their efforts to rationalize work, companies weeded out their mavericks and tried to put them someplace apart: in R&D facilities, in innovation centers, in skunkworks—anywhere but within the main organization. While this approach might work for the creative personality, it doesn't work for the company. Their thinking style brings a type of diversity that's needed in the main organization to create an optimal climate.

Culture Strategy 8:
Improve or Change the System

The notion that people have preferred problem-solving styles was first advanced in the early 1970s by Michael Kirton at the Occupational Research Centre in London. Kirton speculated that there are two principal styles of creativity: adaptive (those who prefer to improve the system) and innovative (those who prefer to change the system), and he devised a 33-question survey, the KAI Inventory, to objectively assess an individual's preferred style. Kirton's work led him to observe that most people naturally prefer one style to the other, and that among the general population, preferences are fairly evenly dispersed.

Inside organizations and specific work groups, however, Kirton and his adherents discovered that the mix of creativity styles often gets skewed in ways that are detrimental to the culture. Charles Prather, former manager of DuPont's Center for Innovation and Creativity, frequently uses Kirton's instrument to gain deeper insights into the mix of styles in the companies he works with as an independent consultant.

Because people with an adaptive problem-solving style seek to make an existing system or process better, they are naturally comfortable suggesting and implementing *process* ideas: those that reduce costs, improve productivity, ensure safer procedures. Having worked with and administered the survey to groups of employees in more than 50 large companies, Prather finds that manufacturing groups and human resource groups, to mention two, tend to be populated by people with this orientation. "These people bring high immediate value to any business," says Prather. "Without them, the business would quickly fail."

By contrast, innovative problem-solvers seek to change the system. These folks tend to exhibit the maverick style. They have no problem coming up with ideas that might change the fundamental nature of the business. Marketing staffers and research and development scientists consistently exhibit this style.

By better understanding these styles, starting with your own, you can staff teams and functional areas more appropriately, avoid the pitfalls of inappropriate staffing, and better capitalize on the talent pool you have. Asked for clues as to a person's likely KAI score, Prather uses the example of a person's wallet. If you organize the bills in your wallet sequentially, and if you know without looking how much money you have in your wallet at any given time, chances are your creativity style is adaptive. If you haven't got a clue as to how much is in there, much less how it's arranged, your style is likely to be innovative.

From a cultural perspective, what's most important is that leaders and managers at all levels (and especially those in human resources) understand the importance of achieving the right mix in creativity styles. As in a marriage where each partner compensates for the other's weaknesses or strengths, so too in work settings. Team problems call for a variety of problem-solving styles. So does the corporate-wide challenge to grow via innovation. Every company needs a balance and blending of styles. Groups populated by too many innovators won't execute well. And groups where the innovative style is absent or sorely lacking won't necessarily surface bold, stretch goals or ideas.

People invariably do best when they are in jobs that require the problem-solving style they naturally prefer. "When you see someone struggling under their job responsibilities like a donkey under a heavy pack," says Prather, "the cause can usually be traced to a great mismatch between the problem-solving style demanded by the job and the one the jobholder prefers. The greater the mismatch, the more unproductive energy must be expended to cope with the job's ill-fitting demands, leaving less available energy to do the job."

By extension, appointing a person exhibiting strong adaptive characteristics to be the company's innovation champion would be a mistake. Conversely, appointing someone with a strong innovative style to be responsible for the company's quality initiative would not be a good fit.

Culture Strategy 9:
Examine Your Attitude Regarding Innovation and Individual Contribution

Abraham Lincoln once said that God must love ordinary people because he made so many of them. Lincoln, were he alive today, might have been talking about rank and file employees. Fact is, most organizations consistently underestimate the innovative potential of the broad middle class of ordinary people inside organizations. They don't know how to stimulate or harvest their ideas, and they go to extraordinary measures to design jobs where thinking is essentially eliminated altogether.

Not so at companies that are rethinking their unspoken but prevailing belief systems to accelerate bottom-up innovations. Consider how these ordinary contributors did extraordinary deeds.

Starbucks' popular Frappuccino drink came not from the product development wizards at headquarters, but from a few regional managers who got the idea literally while sharing a cup of coffee. Almost as a joke, they experimented with a variety of formulations until they got universal "mmm, that's really good" approval from coworkers and customers, only then sharing the idea with top brass in Seattle.

Faced with a growing number of lawsuits, DuPont's legal department looked for ways to accomplish more in less time with fewer resources. They introduced new, more efficient case-management systems and databases that saved $15 million in its first year. Better yet: the new system decreased the average time required to resolve a case by 44 percent.

More and more companies are realizing that the heart and soul of their culture resides in the everyday attitudes and aptitudes of their regular contributors. To achieve growth, these firms are establishing systems that embed idea management into the fiber of the organization.

Culture Strategy 10:
Identify and Develop Champions

Champions are those people in your organization who are adept at shepherding, developing, and nurturing ideas toward the goal line of launching them into the marketplace or implementing them within the firm.

Champions, who are not to be confused with the innovation leader of the entire firm, also have to have experience and credibility within the organization. They need a sense of how the business operates, how it creates value for the customer, and who to see to get things done. They also need an uncanny ability to overcome obstacles and solve problems. They need to know how to get approval for ideas, to "work the system," and to find resources needed to make the idea go, including facilities, equipment, budget, information, and people.

Champions must also be good at networking, both inside and outside the organization. They need to have a good "feel" for the market environment, for what customers will and will not respond to, and they must have experience commercializing new ideas. They need selling skills, persuasion skills, the ability to convince and get buy-in from those who may be opposed to their ideas, and an ability to motivate people who don't report to them. They also need to be able to inspire the best work from technical people and specialists and to orchestrate cross-functional teams toward goal achievement. Champions often personalize the project and infuse uncommon enthusiasm in the teams they lead by their personal example of persistence and passion.

Think of champions as idea quarterbacks. In innovation-adept companies, champions are in charge of the interdisciplinary or cross-functional teams that translate ideas into reality. Bill Steere, former chairman of Pfizer Pharmaceuticals, was credited with spearheading an initiative in that company that continues to bear fruit after he retired in 2000. Steere supplemented the well-defined, well-articulated hierarchies at Pfizer by promoting creation of a wide variety of interdisciplinary teams to manage special projects. Steere believed that a good team could do things faster than a hierarchy could, but only if it was led by effective champions and was empowered to make decisions and move ahead without a lot of bureaucratic red tape.

"You can't have a leaderless matrix because then the team wanders," says Steere. "But if you have a good quarterback for the matrix, they can do things fast, convince the hierarchy that it's the right thing to do."

How important are champions to executing innovation? Gifford Pinchot III, author of *Intrapreneuring: Why You Don't Have to Leave the Corporation to Become an Entrepreneur,* and an early proponent of the Innovation Movement, has studied many hundreds of cases of innovations in his work as a consultant. Pinchot said that he "has yet to find a success that happened without a strong champion," whom he has named "intrapreneur."

Does your business unit or company have enough champions to effectuate change? If your answer is yes, you and your firm are fortunate. If your answer is no, remember this: Champions are made, not born. They get better with practice, by observing other champions at work, and being mentored by them. But because they are so vital, you may also need to alter the way your firm recruits people, so that instead of looking for people who think, act, and behave "just like the rest of us," you go outside the mold and attract a few mavericks and champions.

Culture Strategy 11:
Identify and Recruit Innovators

What things did you make as a child? What was a stumbling block you encountered while working on a problem, and how did you handle it? Do you like to "perfect the system" or "change the system"?

If you are applying for a job at an ever-growing list of innovation-adept companies, these are not just random questions. They are asked for a specific purpose: to determine your innovation style, and how your skills and abilities meet needs of having the proper mix of mavericks, champions, and contributors—both now and in the future. To foster ongoing innovation, human resource professionals are beginning to ask questions that 3M has been a trendsetter in evolving.

At 3M, a team of company recruiters, human resource specialists, and members of the technical community interviewed 25 of the most prolific company inventors. Their mission: to identify signs of innovative potential to use in screening job applicants. These company inventors exhibited characteristics that have since become the basis for hiring practices; they:

- *Are creative:* they ask questions constantly, like looking for solutions, exploring new areas

- *Have broad interests:* are eager to learn, like exploring ideas with others, have hobbies, are multidisciplinary

- *Are problem-solvers:* have an experimental style, "do it first, explain later," are not afraid to make mistakes, take multiple approaches to problems, willing to do the unexpected

- *Are self-motivated/energized:* are self-starters/driven, results oriented, have a passion about what they do, take initiative

- *Have a strong work ethic:* are committed, work in cycles, flexible, not structured work habits, and are tenacious

- *Are resourceful:* are able to network to solve problems and get information, and able to get things done through others.

Like 3M, many companies profile people who now work at the firm to identify (and hire) people that best "fit the mold." That's fine if you want to continue the status quo. But if you find yourself needing to change the mold to create the right mix of mavericks, champions, and regular contributors to accelerate innovation, then you may have to alter the balance slightly to include different personality types.

Designing Your 21st Century Approach to an Innovation-Adept Culture

What systems and practices are in place at your firm that continuously open your culture to experimentation, taking a contrary view, and showing initiative to marshal evidence that an idea has merit? If you're a manager, you can take steps to create a conducive culture today, rather than waiting for others. Simply by starting the next meeting by revealing a mistake you made recently and describing what you learned from the experience is a small step toward a healthier climate.

As you reflect on the important issues of this chapter, our suggestion is that you take pen in hand and jot down the things you personally feel are barriers to innovation within your company. (Later, it will be informative for you to compare what items you came up with to those that other groups polled came up with.) Also that you turn the subheadings of this chapter into questions for you and your innovation process design team to reflect on. For example:

1. How would you describe your organization's culture: its values, beliefs, behaviors? What stories get told around your firm that encourage innovative behavior, and what stories get told that do the opposite?

2. How big a gap exists between what you believe to be your firm's optimal climate for innovation and the one that exists presently?

3. Does your business unit or company have the right balance of people at all levels of the organization to ensure a conducive culture?

4. What barriers are responsible for blocking increased innovative output?

5. Do you have enough people who can champion ideas? Who can lead teams to come forth with new products and business models?

There's no question that culture is a key ingredient at innovation-adept companies, and that moving the growth needle via innovation will mean taking steps to address cultural issues. But after you've pondered the above questions, don't wait till you have created the perfect culture to move forward with your innovation blueprint. No culture is perfect, and all that we've studied are "works in progress."

As we move on to another key topic—how your firm "handles" ideas—you'll see the cultural implications at every turn. Especially as it relates to the opening question of the next chapter.

CHAPTER 4

Empowering the Idea Management Process

The old Borg-Warner would have said you can't organize
the innovation process, that's impossible.
The new Borg-Warner says "we have a process for everything else,
let's have one for innovation."

—Simon Spencer

Borg-Warner's 1st Innovation Champion

If someone in your company has an idea, do they know what to do with it? Ask around the office and see what you come up with. People are often not sure how to answer this question, and their responses are full of a lot of "ifs" and "they could try" and "probably it would be best to."

When InnovationNetwork, a global consortium of innovation-minded thinkers and practitioners, recently surveyed 8000 subscribers to its Monday Morning Wake Up Brain e-zine on this issue, few well-defined responses were received. "We had some sort of program," was a common response, "I'm not sure whatever became of it."

Such is the state of how ideas are encouraged, captured, developed, prioritized, funded and otherwise *managed* in companies today. By contrast, the small but growing number of Innovation Vanguard firms have made idea management the centerpiece of their unending drive for new revenues.

What Idea Management Systems Can Do for Your Firm

Idea systems can help your firm make innovation a discipline. They can help make the hunt for new possibilities every department's business, rather than a select few. And they can help to involve broader participation among managers and employees.

Idea systems do not replace existing methods of opportunity discovery and idea development. Instead they become an adjunct to them. They don't attempt to make end runs around traditional departments and processes involved in new services, products, or strategies. Instead, they invigorate them to get better. "We were not about to abandon our product development processes," notes Robert Goss, innovation czar at appliance maker Whirlpool Corporation, based in Benton Harbor, Michigan.

As good as the processes were, they weren't driving growth. The firm was barely growing at the rate of the Gross Domestic Product, margins were razor thin, and consumers had scant reason to replace existing appliances with new ones that lacked noticeable value-adding benefits. What to do?

Whirlpool Corporation's newly conceived Innovation Team has begun to change all of that. "We are supplementing those processes with radical innovation," says Goss. "We are looking to invent products that never existed before and new marketing and distribution channels that create whole new businesses."

Whirlpool Corporation's new approach is but one of a number of new systems companies are using to get serious about managing ideas. In this chapter we'll explore eight distinct models of idea management. After that, we'll offer ten suggestions to help you put your own system in place. But let's begin with a model that's at least a hundred years old.

Model 1: The Suggestion System

Kathryn Kridel, a lead attendant on American Airlines transcontinental flights to and from Europe, noticed that planes were stocked with 200-gram cans of caviar, an ample amount for the full complement of

---

Idea Management Models

1. The Suggestion System Model

2. The Continuous Improvement Model

3. The Open Door Model

4. The New Venture Team Model

5. The Incubator Model

6. The Top-Line, All-Enterprise Model

7. The Innovation Team Model

8. The Innovation Catalyst Model

---

13 passengers in the first-class cabin. But even when the cabin was almost empty, Kridel and her colleagues still had to open the large cans, which cost the airline $250 each, much of it going to waste. Kridel's "aha!" require vendors to supply caviar in smaller cans, so that when the passenger load was light, less caviar would be wasted.

Kridel's idea, which she wrote up and submitted to the company's suggestion program, was implemented shortly thereafter. It reduced American's annual caviar consumption by $567,000, and Kridel was awarded a bonus of $50,000. Coworkers jokingly dubbed her the "caviar queen."

American Airlines is one of 6000 organizations in the United States with similar programs. Ideas like Kridel's save companies $2 billion per year, or an average of $6224 for each implemented suggestion. Popular with manufacturers, employee involvement programs, as they are also called, have been adopted by a wide range of service companies and government agencies as well.

Dismissed by some as a throwback to a bygone era, suggestion systems have fallen into disuse in many firms. Others are reviving them. "The systems coming out now are computerized, professionally managed, and have real incentives," says John Holland, former president of the Employee Involvement Association. "Today's workers are more educated than in the past, and companies realize that people on the front lines often know more about what's going on than they do."

Suggestion programs provide employees an organized system through which to submit ideas and to have those ideas considered by a panel of dispassionate reviewers, who accept or reject them depending on pre-established criteria from management. The rationale is that the workers are often in the best position to see where something could be improved, in every area from health and safety standards to the best kind of vending machines. Most often, the emphasis is on new ways to cut costs.

Traditionally, suggestion programs have rewarded submissions with monetary rewards. In a recent year, contributors received $165 million in cash, according to the Employee Involvement Association in Fairfax, Virginia. While some companies give employees points redeemable for merchandise, the standard award is 10 percent of the amount saved during the first year of the idea's implementation. Many pay a nominal fee for successful ideas that have no quantifiable payoff. Managers are usually exempted from the programs, although some firms reward them with bonuses if one of their subordinates turns in a winning recommendation.

American Airlines' Suggestion Program   Under American's program, flight attendants, mechanics, and 85,000 other employees (but not managers) can contribute ideas. Called IdeAAs, the program generates 17,000 ideas a year, of which 8,000 are seriously considered, and 25 percent of these are implemented. At the airline's Dallas headquarters, a department of 47 full-time employees manages the ideas and makes sure the best ones get implemented. In a recent year, the program saved the airline $36 million.

Alan Robinson and Sam Stern, in their book, *Corporate Creativity: How Innovation and Improvement Actually Happen*, examined American Airlines' program in depth. They found the biggest source of proposals to IdeAAs has always been maintenance employees, and their ideas make up 47 percent of the system's cost savings. Some mechanics earn as much as $100,000 for their suggestions.

While interviewing one particularly entrepreneurial duo in American's program, the researchers discovered their ingenious method of locating money-saving ideas. One man who worked in accounting would periodically run a check of maintenance expenditures, scanning for expensive parts that were used in quantity. When he found any that fit the pattern, he would alert his coworker, a lead mechanic for the large jets. This worker would then pull these parts off the aircraft, examine them for patterns of wear or damage, and the two would brainstorm ways to reinforce them to prolong their usefulness. If the mechanic felt American was paying too much for the part, the duo would search for less expensive alternatives.

"This team's work is precisely what IdeAAs is rewarding," observe Robinson and Stern. Although such cost-cutting zeal is obviously useful to the airline's bottom line, to these experts, it represents a giant missed opportunity: the potential additional creativity American could be tapping but isn't.

"The great number of ideas that people have but don't pursue—because they don't think that they will generate cost savings or don't believe that the cost savings can be measured—are a limitation to all such programs that rely on monetary rewards to encourage cost saving ideas," note these researchers, concluding, "the more a firm focuses on cost savings, the less likely it is to pursue ideas whose cost savings are not immediately apparent."

Limitations of the Suggestion Model Suggestion programs have been around for at least 100 years. They have proved that individual contributors have ideas that can help companies cut costs, enhance safety, aid job satisfaction, and raise productivity. Because they have been used for so many years by a wide variety of companies, their track record is proven. Setting one up in your company is a matter of benchmarking companies that have them and learning from their vast experience.

The limitations of this idea management model are low participation rates, requirement of a staff to manage them, and the fact that most are confined to searching for money-saving process ideas.

Most of these programs are not designed to stimulate new thinking about revenue growth. Typically they perpetuate the functional fiefdoms, cultural values, and prejudices of traditionally run organizations: That product and service ideas are the exclusive province of specific departments; and that "front-line" workers are not expected to have growth-enhancing top-line ideas.

Traditionally run suggestion programs have a low reputation among most members of the Innovation Movement because of these limitations. Such generalizations may unfairly limit this model's potential and overlook the positive experiences that have occurred in the lives of thousands of contributors who have received recognition for their creativity. It also ignores those organizations that have used suggestion programs to manage more than merely cost-savings ideas.

Model 2: Continuous Improvement Teams

Similar to suggestion programs, the Continuous Improvement Model primarily focuses on cost savings. But here the scope is much more likely to go beyond process savings to include product improvements, safety, workplace, and quality ideas rather than just cost savings. And unlike suggestion programs that focus on motivating individual contributors to come forward with their ideas, Continuous Improvement Model systems rely on team collaboration. Sometimes called Kaizen Teams, (*kaizen* is the Japanese word for continuous improvement), they mostly focus on incremental, rather than substantial or breakthrough process on product improvements. Nevertheless, when these seemingly small, continuous tweaks produced by firm's rank and file workers are added up, they can be substantial in their bottom-line impact.

Dana Corporation's Program   One company that has mastered the Continuous Improvement Model is Toledo, Ohio-based Dana Corporation, one of the world's largest independent suppliers to vehicle manufacturers and the replacement parts market. The $16 billion company operates 320 facilities in 33 countries and employs more than 82,000 people.

Joseph M. Magliochetti, Dana's chairman, notes that each Dana employee is encouraged to submit two ideas per month, and that the company strives for 80 percent implementation. These ideas, which arise from frequent team brainstorming sessions at the plant level, generate more than two million ideas per year about how to improve quality, productivity, safety, and efficiency. For example:

- A Dana worker in the company's Brazil plant takes continuous improvement so seriously he reported an average of two ideas per day.

- Workers at the Columbia, Missouri, plant came up with ideas that dramatically impacted the assembly process for Isuzu Rodeo rear axles.

- Workers at Dana's Elizabethtown, Kentucky, frame plant came up with an idea involving a minor process change that allowed the automatic loading of steel sheets into a forming press. This effectively led to the reassignment of six workers and a quicker way of getting the product to the customer.

- A Dana assembly worker got the idea to install two bicycle mirrors opposite his work station so he could double-check an assembly without flipping over the 90-pound object, resulting in a 25 percent productivity gain, and a rather pleased employee.

"We believe our people, those doing the job day after day, are the true experts in their area," notes Magliochetti. "It's our duty to listen carefully, encourage their participation, and garner their support."

Limitations of the Continuous Improvement Model Dana's program of keeping the process improvement juices flowing in its factory workers is based on the Japanese model, which has been used by Toyota and other firms to create higher quality and more reliable products at lower cost. Yet, if customers perceive those products as stodgy or unexciting, continuous improvement methods do little to enhance customer-perceived value and therefore do little to rev up top-line growth. (Toyota's quality initiatives have been so effective, however, that the manufacturer continues to gain market share globally despite a generally stodgy line of automobiles.) If a company is preoccupied with efficiency-enhancement and cost-savings ideas, it tends not to be equally preoccupied with aggressively entering new markets, developing new customer groups, using breakthrough technology, and offering superior design.

To drive growth, firms need to do more than continually, incrementally improve processes and products. They need to further restructure their idea management systems on an enterprise-wide scale to capture the passion and creativity in their ranks.

Model 3: The Open Door Policy

The Open Door Model, while widely varying in its practice, is generally one in which the leader, whether division or business unit head, chairman, or CEO, invites contributors to bypass the chain of command and come directly to him or her with any ideas they might have.

The Open Door Model has long been used by leaders who want to communicate the value they place on ideas and to provide a "court of last resort" for frustrated mavericks. Many of the Innovation Vanguard firms studied for this book use it in conjunction with much more comprehensive idea management processes as yet another way of keeping the firm's culture open to new ideas. "We have an open door policy that any employee anywhere can go to any leader in the company that they feel would best address their issue," says EDS's Melinda Lockhart. But we'll see that EDS's methods are much greater.

Disney's Gong Show In his early years as chairman and CEO of Disney, Michael Eisner began hosting idea-pitching Gong Shows, named after a long-since canceled television program on which amateur contestants would sing, dance, or tell jokes until one of a panel of judges banged on a huge gong, signaling that that person's time was up. The show's winning contestant was the one who performed the longest.

Disney's interpretation of the Open Door Model works like this: Any contributor who thinks he or she has a good idea (and can't get anyone else to go along) can show up at a thrice-yearly Gong Show and attempt to sell the idea to representatives of top management. Despite the humorous name, these sessions give Disneyites an "open door" to propose top-line ideas to top-line people. Even ideas that advocate Disney get into whole new businesses are fair game. Disney lore has it that the idea for the firm's retail shops was proposed at a Gong Show by contributor Steve Burke.

Disney's version of the Open Door Model of Idea Management may come off as slightly demeaning, but Eisner proudly mentions it in his autobiography, *Work in Progress*.

Pros and Cons of the Open Door Model Open Door is best used in conjunction with other, more comprehensive idea management programs. Open Door models provide a much-needed safety valve for creative persons with bigger-than-continuous improvement ideas to receive a forum. What is amazing is that this approach, while comparatively rudimentary and primitive to other systems companies are designing today, actually works as often as it does.

One environment in which Open Door seems to work well is in

those where the leader is a bit of a maverick himself or herself. Richard Branson, chairman of London-based Virgin Group, fits this description to a tee. In the past decade alone, Virgin has created nearly 200 new businesses, from entertainment superstores to theater chains, from an airline to radio stations, and from a passenger train service to a bridal planning chain.

This latter business was proposed to Branson by Ailsa Petchey, a Virgin Atlantic flight attendant. Petchey, soon to wed and strapped for time, decidedly didn't like how she had been treated in her experience shopping for bridal products and services. She took Branson at his word that his door was always open and presented a whole new business: a one-stop wedding planning shop. Branson liked the idea so much he asked Petchey to become the founder of Virgin Bride, and he provided the seed money.

Model 4: New Venture Teams

The goal of the New Venture Team Model is decidedly not cost-saving ideas, not incremental improvements, and not process innovations. Rather, the goal is more apt to be surfacing (and funding) unconventional product, service, or strategy ideas that have the potential to be breakthroughs.

Procter & Gamble's Corporate New Ventures Approach   In 1994, Procter & Gamble formed a task force called Corporate New Ventures (CNV), an autonomous idea lab whose mission was to encourage new product ideas from P&G's 110,000-person workforce, fund the most promising, shelter them from the firm's labyrinthine product development system, and speed them to market launch.

Once CNV latched onto an idea it believed had potential, it put the idea under quick scrutiny, analyzing market potential and cost information for feasibility, and if it decided to go ahead, the project was launched within days. The CNV team had the authority to tap any resource in the company to bring a new product to market, including the brainpower of the company's engineers, scattered in 23 sites around the globe. In short order, CNV put 58 products into the market, one of them the cleaning product, Swiffer, which went from concept to on-the-shelf product in a record-setting 10 months and has since become, if not quite a breakthrough for the company, then something quite close.

Nortel's Phantom Stock Approach   Like P&G, Toronto-based Nortel Networks formed a special new venture board, with a twist that management hoped would spur faster results. Nortel promised to award entrepreneurial employees with "phantom stock" when they volunteered for special, high-risk projects. Nortel agreed to "buy" these projects as if they were companies, in a sort of internal initial public offering. Team participants were to get paid in chits redeemable for cash when a product was finished and again after it had been on the market for a year. Some 17 products were developed under the program, but then, like Procter & Gamble's CNV, the initiative was suddenly discontinued during a severe downturn in the telecom sector in the early 2000s.

EDS's New Venture Team Model   Not every new venture team disappears so quickly. One of the leading practitioners and advancers of this model is Electronic Data Systems of Plano, Texas.

When Dick Brown took the helm at EDS, cultural assessments and his own observations indicated there were a number of deep-seated barriers that had to be addressed: no formal recognition within the corporation that "thought leadership" was important; no clear vision or strategy; no investment commitment for innovation; no new ideas that had any guarantee of payback; no investment governance; no channel for good ideas; no ability to go from idea to execution in a seamless planned manner; organizational structure that is complex and fragmented; no single accountability for innovation leadership.

"We rewarded stewardship, not entrepreneurship," sums up Melinda Lockhart, EDS's innovation maven. "Our culture was, 'you take care of your people and you take care of your P&L and you nurture and be kind and we'll reward and recognize you.' But if you came up with great ideas, well, there was no compensation for that. In the culture that exists at EDS today, it's not that we've stopped rewarding stewardship. Rather, it's that these forces coexist and are better balanced."

The centerpiece of EDS's idea management system is a program called Idea2Reality. It operates as an internal market, attracting ideas from employees and funding development of the most promising submissions. Idea2Reality is decidedly not a suggestion program. It seeks growth-producing new products, which EDS terms "service offerings," but significant process improvements are welcomed as well.

In designing Idea2Reality, the team sought input from venture capitalists, as well as other companies that had previously introduced this approach to idea management. These organizations had already gained experience in the best ways to attract attention of a globally dispersed employee base, and in how to select ideas for funding, support "intrapreneurs," and otherwise manage the process.

To make it easy to submit an idea, EDS employees from Bangkok to Berlin to Birmingham are encouraged to submit their ideas via the company's intranet. Once an idea is received, a member of the 15-person Idea2Reality support staff then contacts the person to help scope, refine, and further articulate the idea. The Plano-based Idea2Reality staff is really a cross-functional team of business and technology experts dedicated to thinking through the idea and shoring up the business plan for that idea. The team also seeks feedback from appropriate EDS Innovation Fellows who have been awarded this title based on their prior contributions to the company's top and bottom line.

Next, an executive team reviews the submission and decides whether to award seed funding. This team, which meets twice a month, is chaired by the chief technology officer who is also in charge of innovation corporate-wide. Initial funding can be as little as several thousand dollars. The suggesting employee is often invited to further develop the idea at an EDS incubator facility. There the funding goes toward software, market research, airplane tickets for convening focused discussions on the idea, and whatever else is necessary for the ideas' initiator to research the idea during a 30-day period. As with idea incubators that sponsor and assist start-up entrepreneurial firms, the initiator is freed from much of the administrative tasks, which are handled by the Idea2Reality support staff.

At the end of the development phase, the Investment Opportunity Team, a new venture-funding panel composed of key decision makers from EDS's various business units, reviews ideas that have been submitted. At this juncture, the funding team might decide to reject the idea, award further seed funding, or fully fund the idea for full-scale accelerated development. For "white space" opportunities (those that don't have an obvious home in a particular strategic business unit), a fourth choice is available. The innovator might be given the green light to seek a joint venture or licensing agreement with an outside firm, or, in rare cases, to establish a new business.

One final design feature of EDS's approach is how this initiative coexists with the "normal innovation" service offering within each business unit. What Idea2Reality does is to serve as an extracurricular funding vehicle that can develop breakthroughs without the business units having to take a big hit on their P&Ls in order to fund riskier, longer-payoff type ventures that might occur in the white space between business units.

Don't Try This One in a Hurry The New Venture Model of idea management is often the epitome of an ad hoc, "let's do something in a hurry" approach to innovation. Lacking ideas and in a market slump? Form a new venture team; that's the answer. (At Nortel, the pattern was reversed. Times were flush in the late 1990s when it announced the "phantom stock" approach.) If a new venture team approach tries to do end-runs around existing research and development processes without first addressing the cultural issues necessary to ensure acceptance of the team's work, it will almost certainly fail.

Neither Nortel or Procter & Gamble have embraced an all-enterprise approach to innovation. Like so many others that have haphazardly embraced the New Venture Model, both achieved initial results. But corporate politics and shifting priorities soon intervened.

Model 5: The Incubator Lab

The Incubator Model of Idea Management gained popularity along side the dot-com bubble of the late 1990s and lost favor just as fast. Before it was over, companies from Cargill to Ford jumped on the bandwagon. Beneath the hype, the basic idea of incubators was not too different from the skunkworks approach (named after the L'il Abner cartoon) pioneered by Lockheed during World War II to rapidly develop and launch new aircraft by forming small, dedicated teams separate from the bureaucracy.

Xerox's Blue Sky Incubator Xerox's famed Palo Alto Research Center (PARC) is an example of how the incubator model was supposed to work but didn't. The Palo Alto, California, center, one of seven labs owned by the company, was given a mandate to do "blue sky" exploration of new technologies, even if they didn't have an immediate relationship to the company's current products. Unfortunately for Xerox, while this unit developed numerous technological advances, the folks in the rest of the company never commercialized their products for Xerox.

In its existence over three decades, PARC developed a number of exciting technological advances: the computer mouse, the graphic user interface on which all PCs rely, and numerous others. But instead of benefiting Xerox, they benefited start-ups such as Apple Computer, Adobe Systems, and 3Com instead. Finally, in a desperate move for survival, Xerox attempted to sell PARC in 2002.

The idea behind PARC, as with other incubators and skunkworks, is that a separate facility can come up with ideas and simply toss them over the wall for the main organization to implement or take to market. One invention (laser imaging) made it successfully out of PARC to become a breakthrough new business for the company, and it succeeded because the person who championed it in the laboratory also championed it in the company. Robert Adams moved with it and drove its development through engineering, manufacturing, marketing, and sales. And that's exactly what this approach must have to be successful—champions with enough clout and passion, as Peter Drucker famously noted, must be "monomaniacs on a mission," if the idea is going to make it to implementation and market acceptance.

Model 6: The Top-Line, All-Enterprise Approach

As companies challenge their bias that only senior-level people can have senior-level ideas, they are realizing the untapped potential of regular contributors in their organizations. People whose jobs probably do not have anything to do with new product or service development often "just happen to think up ideas" that aren't process improvements at all, which is what most traditional suggestion systems actively solicit and reward. What to do with their ideas for new products and services that might just drive growth?

Not long ago, Tom Terry, a lineman for Verizon Corporation in New York City, spotted a potentially dangerous situation and came up with a special tool to prevent it. Terry's invention made its way to Verizon's Champion Program, the company's well-regarded suggestion system. And in a happy accident of circumstances, the tool eventually became CommGuard, a safety-related product that the company now markets to other telecommunications firms.

Why do suggestion systems have to be limited to soliciting incremental-level, cost-saving ideas and those that increase productivity and safety? Answer: They don't! And that brings us to what we'll call the Top-Line, All-Enterprise Model of Idea Management. Its biggest distinction: This model doesn't limit the scope of ideas from individual contributors—it invites them, respects them, and gives everyone a place to take their notions, for the good of the firm.

Appleton Paper's GO Program   While recent, this model is showing results at Appleton Papers, in Appleton, Wisconsin, the world's leading producer of carbonless and thermal papers. Senior managers at employee-owned Appleton saw the need to revamp their idea management methods in the late 1990s for sheer survival. Appleton's thermal papers division operates in a growth market, because its products are used in everything from bar-coded baggage claim tags to lottery tickets. Its other mainstay product, carbonless papers, which once were used in everything from car rental forms to store receipts, are in deep decline.

Out of desperation, the firm created the GO Process, which stands for growth opportunities. "We already had a [suggestion] program for cost-savings ideas," explains Dennis Hultgren, Appleton's director of public affairs. "With GO, we now regularly solicit ideas from everybody in the company. In one year we've gotten over 700 new product ideas from our 2500 employees. These people are out there, they know our technologies and they are perfectly capable of thinking up new uses [for them]. What we've learned is that it's important to bring everybody in on it. Everybody wants to contribute if asked, but not everyone was being asked."

Ideas generated by Appleton employees are evaluated by nine cross-functional teams, each led by a senior manager "spoke owner," who is in charge of championing top prospects to become out-the-door new products. The teams meet several times a month to brainstorm, share insights gleaned from paying investigative visits to other companies, and to keep the momentum going. The nine teams respond to each idea with a "scorecard" that evaluates the idea and gives a detailed explanation of why the product fits or doesn't fit company objectives and available resources.

Once a month, each team's report is presented to the firm's executive committee to determine the status of new product development. While GO is a new approach, it's already helping drive growth. A direct result of the GO Process includes a new digital paper product that has been released in Germany, and the pipeline is filling with other promising new products as well. Says Hultgren: "People want to work for a company that is growing and is willing to try new approaches. This is a whole new way to operate for us."

Limits of the Top-Line, All-Enterprise Model   The obvious limits of this model are the fact that it is so new and has yet to stand the test of time. It could become a "flavor of the month" approach that a company uses in a slack economy but is abandoned when conditions improve. By suddenly implementing an all-enterprise model without training, the danger is that the program generates a torrent of ideas, but then a bottleneck in sifting, sorting, and reaching consensus about which ones to pursue.

To make this one pay off, attention must be devoted to developing the entrepreneurial skills needed to discover and introduce new products and services and to develop new markets. Additional competence will certainly be needed to introduce new products to new markets. Despite these obvious challenges, the All-Enterprise Model has an obvious appeal.

Model 7: Innovation Teams

The gist of this approach is to set up a company-wide network of people with demonstrated skills in innovation and give them very clear marching orders: Go out and find some new ideas that have promise.

Whirlpool's Innovation Team Approach   Until Whirlpool Corporation adopted this unconventional new method of idea management, growth had come to a standstill, profits were falling, its stock price was at an all-time low, and another cyclical downturn was on the horizon. Management had already tried the usual cost-cutting measures, including the decision to trim 10 percent of the company's 60,000 workers.

Making matters worse, arch-competitor Maytag had caught Whirlpool Corporation by surprise when it introduced its pricey front-loading Neptune washing machine and watched it win big with customers. Neptune was a wake-up call for the $10 billion firm, and the embarrassment, combined with poor performance, was just enough to motivate the company leadership to fundamentally redesign its innovation process, not just come up with a me-too new washer.

The result was Whirlpool Corporation's Innovation Team. The 75-member group—an international cross-functional collection of volunteers—was charged by senior management with scouring the world for ideas that could generate business growth.

"We had this internal market of people we weren't tapping into," explains Nancy Snyder, corporate vice president of strategic competency creation. "We wanted to get rid of the 'great man' theory that only one person—the CEO or people close to him—is responsible for innovation."

The Innovation Team, with guidance from Gary Hamel's innovation consultancy, Strategos, sought ideas from every employee, every region and functional area in the firm. It purposefully didn't limit the types of ideas it was looking for. Next the team deliberated on what to do with ideas it received, which led to the group's establishing evaluative criteria. Out of an initial 1100 ideas gleaned, the Innovation Team identified 80 of the most promising, and out of those, they identified 11 to investigate further, finally winnowing to 6 to actively pursue.

One of the six selected was Personal Valet, a new-to-the-world appliance that makes clothes ready to wear by smoothing away wrinkles and cleaning away odors. Another idea was Inspired Chef, which represents a strategy innovation for Whirlpool Corporation's small appliances division, KitchenAid. Noticing that its many new products needed to be demonstrated to busy households (often time-strapped Baby Boomers), Inspired Chef is designed to do exactly that.

Taking a leaf from Tupperware's distribution system, the Inspired Chef program contracts with chefs and culinary-school grads to host cooking class dinner parties in customers' homes. The chef brings all the food and uses KitchenAid's latest feature-enhanced, goof-proof, cooking appliances, from mixers to juicers, to whip up a meal for the dozen or so invited guests. Most importantly, a catalog full of KitchenAid merchandise is prominently displayed, and the chef takes product orders as well.

A year into implementation, Inspired Chef had a full-time staff of seven people, who coordinated 60 instructors teaching classes in six states. While its top-line revenue potential remains to be proven, the Innovation Team approach gives Whirlpool Corporation a continuous, sustainable vehicle for innovation that invigorates traditional processes.

Model 8: Innovation Catalysts

The Innovation Catalyst Model is similar to the one used by Whirlpool Corporation, EDS, and other firms but with one major exception. Under this model, ideas don't leave the division or business unit to be developed elsewhere, at headquarters, say, or in a skunkworks or incubator.

Instead, they are developed, tested for feasibility, analyzed for risk, prototyped with customers, approved (or killed) and ultimately launched and sold by the division or business unit. In addition, the business unit's performance is measured on the basis of how well it carries out this process, and how often.

Citigroup's Catalyst Approach   Citigroup's Innovation Initiative is global in scope, but it's decidedly decentralized in execution. Designed and debuted in 2001, the initiative's goals (to drive revenue growth) have been adopted in most of the 102 countries where the firm has a presence, becoming a well-managed, embedded discipline that promises to become a process breakthrough for the company.

This model is led by the business managers and supported by an Innovation Catalyst, who serves as champion and expediter on a day-to-day basis at the country and regional levels. The i2i approach (idea to implementation) follows a common set of four stages: Idea Generation, Screening and Approval, Fast Implementation, and Knowledge Transfer (Replication). Ideas are ignited and captured from different sources and in different ways. Some come from the simple suggestions of front-office employees, others from structured ideation sessions with clients. Programs like Citibank's Customer of the Month, whereby the key members of a Citibank country's senior team meet with their counterparts from a select customer to brainstorm present and future needs, key changes, and customer service issues, often produce ideas for new products and services. Industry Groups and Service Roundtables also serve to keep the innovation pipeline flowing.

In Citigroup business units, Innovation Catalysts work closely with Magnet Teams, locally empowered cross-functional groups of senior executives that regularly meet to approve ideas on a simultaneous basis and, on several occasions, on the spot. The catalyst doesn't propose new ideas, but instead helps the relationship or product manager prepare a case for the idea, and document due diligence requirements.

These teams have dramatically improved the concept-to-profit cycle for new products, services, and the targeting of new markets. Based on a proprietary prioritization exercise that assesses future business impact, dedicated implementation teams are assigned for rapid implementation of approved ideas into the marketplace.

The results of this approach are visible in several markets that are diversified in size, culture, language, competition, business dynamics, and regulatory environment. Citibank in Trinidad and Tobago is one of the best examples of the success of this approach. In consistently applying this new discipline and with strong local leadership, the new revenues derived from this model were responsible for 30 percent of the total in a recent year. Citibank's unit in one Asian country is so active that it convenes its Magnet team every week, and sometimes twice a week, to review and prioritize ideas that have been proposed.

"The utilization of this simple but solid discipline across 24 geographies has a number of benefits," says Michael Contreras, head of Citigroup Corporate and Investment Banking in Latin America. "It facilitates the empowerment of our local management teams, it reduces bureaucracy and improves speed to the market all at the same time."

Another important capability brought on by the global initiative is a heightened ability to accomplish "success transfer," Citigroup's term for "copying shamelessly and rapidly replicating ideas that were pioneered elsewhere in the organization." In this regard, the Innovation Catalyst Network plays a very critical role in the idea transfer process, and a full-time employee at Network headquarters in Stamford, Connecticut does nothing but help the country business managers gain access to hot ideas that are generating revenue in other parts of the firm.

"What is really important is how fast we create competitive advantage in individual markets," notes Elcio Pereira, the regional champion for Innovation throughout Latin America, and an active player in the Citigroup Innovation Catalyst Network. "It doesn't matter if the knowledge or solution is created in Singapore, South Africa, India, or Venezuela, we all benefit from the synergy of rapid success transfer across the entire organization."

Limitations of the Catalyst Model   Like all models, this one has its strengths and its limitations. It was designed to spur innovation and success transfer within the unique requirements of global financial services companies, where a one-size-fits-all approach to global product rollout clearly wouldn't work, due to differing regulatory requirements in each local market and differing customer requirements.

The catalyst model also works best in highly decentralized firms, where individual business units and regions have autonomy to grow their franchises in the way they deem best.

The only limitation to this model is one that could be claimed of any model: Implementation takes time, and it is critical to have strong, aggressive, entrepreneurial leaders in place who support their catalysts and are active participants in the innovation process. As Citigroup has discovered, it also helps to have at least a small staff in place at headquarters who are responsible for communicating system-wide the exciting ideas that are just beginning to drive growth in other parts of the firm.

Designing Your 21st Century Idea Management Process

Having looked at some of the approaches firms use to manage ideas, how might you establish a process that is right for your company? What are the dos and don'ts, and where best to start?

Start by considering these issues:

- What do we want our idea management process to do for us?

- How do we expect that this design will enable us to meet those objectives?

- How will our idea management system embed innovation into our company such that it becomes "the way we do things around here"?

Here are ten guidelines to keep in mind as you consider how best to empower the process of idea management in your company:

Guideline 1: Assess How Ideas Are Presently Managed

How satisfied are you that it is the best it can be? How often do employees leave to pursue an idea that might have benefited your firm if they'd been able to act on it? What's working well in the many processes already in place?

Guideline 2: The System Should Solicit Ideas from Everybody

The bottom line is this: If you want people's ideas, you've got to ask for them. And then you have to have processes in place to handle the ideas you get.

Innovation Vanguard companies realize that good ideas can come from anywhere, at any time. They can come from the sales force and the service technicians who are out talking and interacting with customers every day. They can come from suppliers who may have ideas that could benefit either you or your competitor, whom they also supply. They can come from your receptionist who's asked questions by callers, and from front-line associates of all stripes. They can come from supervisors, midlevel managers, freelancers, researchers, and even temps (who have a real cross-functional and cross-company view).

They can also come from departing employees who may be disgruntled, and arriving employees who bring fresh approaches and insights. They can come from customers and, yes, they even can come from senior managers. Nobody can attach a meter to the basic idea and determine its potential—at least at first.

Guideline 3: The System Must Be Easy to Use

For an idea management system to be accepted, ease of use turns out to be a critical success factor. Make your system 24/7 accessible to people; when ideas happen, people want to do something with them in a hurry. Their passion is at its peak. Don't make them wait till Monday. Capture them now.

Guideline 4: The System Should Have at Least One Full-time Person to Administer It

An idea system only works if there is a reason for people to record the ideas in an effective way. If it is an additional responsibility for someone with a full-time job already, it will always be a secondary priority

Guideline for Your Own Idea Management System

1. Assess how ideas are presently managed.

2. The system should solicit ideas from everybody.

3. The system must be easy to use.

4. The system should have at least one full-time person to administer it.

5. The system should give people permission to bypass the chain of command.

6. The system should respond promptly to idea contributors.

7. The system should have innovation-savy people in place to review ideas.

8. The system should involve the contributor for whenever possible.

9. The system should give recognition for the very act of contributing, regardless of what happens with the idea.

10. The system should integrate different models to fit your firm's unique culture.

and won't get done properly. Result: Good ideas will be lost, and people won't continue to use it.

Guideline 5: The System Should Give People Permission to Bypass the Chain of Command

Your system should provide an alternative way for ideas to receive a hearing. Permission to bypass the normal chain of command is necessary because a particular employee's "boss" may not see the efficacy of an idea or may not wish that employee to pursue it for fear of "losing" that employee. The manager may stifle an idea that the employee feels strongly about. Unless this safety valve is an accepted part of the system, employees will tend to pursue only those ideas they know will please their immediate managers. A perfect time to publicize this "rule" is when you are implementing your new idea management approach; that way, nobody takes it personally, yet everyone is put on notice that they are no longer the final say when an employee has an idea.

Guideline 6: The System Should Respond Promptly to Idea Contributors

The biggest cause of failure to any system is that it takes too long to get back to people. One system we learned about promises that if an idea hasn't been acknowledged in 20 business days, it automatically goes to the president's desk. A rapid response that says "thanks for the idea, here's what you can expect to happen," provides much needed feedback and encouragement.

Guideline 7: The System Should Have Innovation-savvy People in Place to Review Ideas

The committee or team that reviews the ideas must understand that most new ideas seem like duds at first. If looked at through traditional ROI measures, few make sense. The most common mistake is to assess new ideas that need significant funding through the conventional metrics of financial projections and planning. If the idea is a potential breakthrough, it *creates* the future, rather than just extrapolates a future that is like the present.

If the idea is truly original, it solves a problem the customer may not even be aware of having or consider to be a problem. The idea will create a new market, as we'll see later in this book. That's why you have to carefully select the people who will sit in judgment of ideas. They must have a feel for the future and be broad-based and diverse in experience. They must have experience in championing ideas, must be able to be imaginative, to boldly challenge industry assumptions and holy grails. They must themselves be able to imagine not just new products, but new markets as well. Choose carefully!

Guideline 8: The System Should Involve the Contributor Whenever Possible

It is critical how this team responds to ideas it can't use right now. You'll need to teach your people how to give and receive feedback on their ideas. If we reject some ideas out of hand without providing an adequate justification, we lose the good will and creativity of individuals.

If ideas are rejected in such a way that employees lose face, you lose not only them, but all the people around them.

If ideas are converted into reality without the idea-spawner being rewarded, this is apt to stifle future ideas. Supervisors need to be able to recognize good ideas when they see them and to access them when needed.

Guideline 9: The System Should Give Recognition for the Very Act of Contributing, Regardless of What Happens with the Idea

This recognition can range from a simple verbal thank you or personalized e-mail to naming people at staff or company meetings to plaques or certificates. Acknowledgement will increase the participation rate.

Guideline 10: The System Should Integrate Different Models to Fit Your Firm's Unique Culture

Finally, in designing your idea management system, you'll want to borrow from the best, but invent your own. None of these models are perfect by any means, and the more you examine them, the more you'll see how much they overlap. None are complete in themselves, and can be "mixed and matched" to produce a stronger overall approach.

Most important, none of the systems we've looked at are "plug and play" ready for implementation in another company. Benchmarking for the purpose of importing another company's system into your own will not work. You and your colleagues will do well to develop your own. By addressing these guidelines, you'll achieve an idea management process that will drive growth for years to come. And what's more, you'll be ready to actively search for opportunities, which is the subject of the next chapter.

CHAPTER 5

Mining the Future

Making predictions is very difficult,
particularly about the future.
—Yogi Berra

What methods do you and your company employ to detect changes that could spell doom—if appropriate action isn't taken—or boom, if they are? How do you look for "white space" opportunities, those that don't fall neatly into the purview of present operating units? How satisfied are you with your process for mining the future?

Many firms are tempted to put off rethinking and revamping this part of their innovation strategy. Unless their backs are clearly against the wall, they point to recent quarterly performance and say, "we aren't doing that badly, just look." Or "we know we need to improve our processes in that area, but right now we've got a lot on our plate that is more pressing."

Listen to the head of a mid-sized specialty chemical company describe what happened to him.

"We felt we had the [market] niche sewn up because of our strong relationship with a leading customer, a textile manufacturer," said this CEO. "Then a competitor came out with a less expensive substitute. Their product didn't do everything ours did, but it did everything our customer needed. Within months we had lost the account, and no matter how hard we tried, we couldn't get back in."

The company eventually recovered, but the loss of that leading customer cost five years of profits. In hindsight, the signs were all there: Articles in trade journals about the new competitor. Testing of the new product by independent labs and positive reports in the technical literature. Even industry rumors about government subsidies enabling the new competitor to enter the market with lower prices. Looking back, this chastened leader and his senior team asked themselves how this could have happened.

It happened because the company's method of mining the future—of collecting and creatively analyzing trends—was inadequate in an industry with high clockspeed. Discontinuous changes aren't some idle, academic concept. They happen. Disruptive technologies don't just happen to other companies in other industries, they happen in all industries today, and they happen faster than ever before.

A reactive, linear approach won't cut it. Leaving it up to the strategic planning department won't do. Saving it for the annual offsite isn't enough. To respond in a timely manner to changing customer needs and wants, to anticipate what your customers will want in the future, takes serious effort. It needs to be systematic and disciplined. We're not talking about predicting the future but rather not being blindsided by it. And being early to recognize opportunity, regardless of whether you and your firm choose to move first to exploit that opportunity or not. Later in this chapter, we'll explore how innovation-adept firms operate differently. Let's start by going behind the scenes at one of our Innovation Vanguard companies to gain a few practical insights.

Filling the Funnel at Royal Dutch/Shell

In 1996, Tim Warren was executive vice president for exploration and production at Royal Dutch/Shell, one of the world's largest companies. As he observed the growth patterns, Warren decided his division was not innovative enough, that it was overly focused on incremental process improvements and needed more entrepreneurial zeal. He was determined to do something about it. The result was a new approach to idea management that came to be called GameChanger.

After the first two years of GameChanger, Shell's new approach was working so well that other divisions within the company decided to set up their own versions. Within Shell Chemicals, the company's third largest division, a six-person team looks for ways to exploit new and existing technologies and asks "how can we do this business in a different way, how can we change the rules of the game?"

One program manager does nothing but scan the horizon for potential discontinuities. He manages a global network of volunteer "scanners" who read industry journals, attend conferences (the odder the better), and report on regulatory, societal, technological, and global trends and changes. When something looks interesting, "deep divers" run database searches to assess what is going on and feed their insights to the scenario planning process.

Shell Chemical's futurist team is more than an early warning system. Nor is it a think tank for producing reports that never get read. Instead, its work is all about "filling the funnel" with growth-spawning opportunities. As such, GameChanger is linked to an internal venture capital process that solicits, sorts, selects, and sometimes funds promising white space opportunities, and nurtures them into new products, services, processes, technologies, and capabilities.

A big chunk of GameChanger leader Dave Austgen's time is devoted to soliciting ideas from division employees around the world and gaining buy-in for the approach. "We try to get face time in the plants to make presentations about what our unit is up to," says Austgen. "We tell as many people as we can that we want their ideas. We believe these ideas can literally come from anywhere and anybody." A quarterly newsletter reports on hot projects and encourages managers, technologists, and individual contributors to submit their ideas over the company's intranet, which are discussed every Wednesday among the GameChanger team.

"We get 50 proposals a year," says Austgen. "We never reject an idea outright. We focus on enriching the contributor's idea. We don't want to dismiss anybody. We want to help people think through the ideas themselves, and we help them work through the process. We have found that the people who come up with an idea are the best champion of that idea. We team them with a member of the GameChanger group, who becomes their coach, helping them think like an entrepreneur."

Since the cycle time in the chemical industry is generally 5 to 15 years, it's too early to truly assess the impact of GameChanger on the division's growth. One promising idea currently in development came from an engineer at a plant in The Netherlands. GameChanger funded the employee's idea, which proposed a new business that would market a waste product generated at that plant. After GameChanger funded initial development work, the brass in corporate headquarters became enthusiastic; this new business is on its way to generating revenue for the corporation.

Taking the Fuzz Out of the Fuzzy Front End

In innovation circles, the "fuzzy front end" refers to activities that come before the formal, well-structured new product process kicks in. It's here that future possibilities and opportunities first come into view, or fail to. "The front end of innovation appears to represent the greatest area of weakness in the innovation process," concludes a study of company practices published in *Research Technology Management*.

Companies like Royal Dutch/Shell are leading the way in revitalizing this vital part of the discipline. You can too.

How Innovation-Adept Companies Mine the Future

At the Innovation Vanguard companies studied for this book, mining the future is a key priority. These companies have an organized, systematic, and continual process in place. As one manager described it, "We are actively seeking to discover new technologies that might become disruptive to our business, or that we can use to disrupt our competitors." The box lists six strategies innovation-adept firms are using:

Mining Strategy 1:
Scan and Monitor the Sources of Opportunity

Many breakthrough innovations have a common, but less-than-obvious attribute: They exploit change. McDonald's Corporation rode lifestyle changes to success as increasingly mobile Americans were eager for inexpensive, fast food of consistent quality. Old Navy, Gap's retail clothing chain, rode the Generation Y demographic wave

Mining the Future

1. Scan and monitor the sources of innovation opportunity.

2. Create a personal future-scan system.

3. Integrate future scanning with your company's idea management system.

4. Assault industry assumptions.

5. Broaden your company's vision.

6. Strategize your place in the first mover, fast follower race.

by providing hip clothing at affordable prices. Federal Express rode a wave of customer demand for time-sensitive parcel delivery that existing freight forwarders hadn't yet noticed.

The types of change are almost endless: global, economic, technological, social, regulatory, and political. Let's look at how a change of the regulatory variety impacted one firm.

How Progressive Made Lemonade from a Regulatory Lemon   Like all auto insurers operating in California in 1988, Ohio-based Progressive Insurance faced a sudden regulatory change. Fed up with the bureaucracy, high prices, and unresponsiveness of auto insurance companies, California voters passed Proposition 103, which regulated these firms and rolled back escalating rates. The law was a huge hit to Progressive's bottom line, forcing the company to give back $60 million in refunds to customers and to reduce its workforce by 19 percent to survive. But what could have been a voter-tossed lemon became instead a chance to make lemonade.

In response, Progressive rethought and completely altered its business model, supplementing its traditional agent distribution network to also sell directly to customers. It now settles claims on the spot rather than indulging in lengthy delays and attracts new customers via its website by posting not only its own rates but the rates of its competitors, even if their rates are cheaper. Result: Progressive enjoys wider profit margins than any other insurer and grew six times faster than the industry as a whole throughout the 1990s.

Mining Strategy 2:
Create Your Personal Future-Scan System

In researching the book *Winning the Innovation Game*, I interviewed and studied people like Federal Express founder Fred Smith, Intel chairman Andrew Grove, polio vaccine pioneer Dr. Jonas Salk, Segway inventor Dean Kamen, and others. I was struck by how systematic they all were in keeping abreast of trends and new ideas. "They are like vacuum cleaners," I wrote. "I would be there to interview them, to understand their success characteristics and they would in turn pepper me with questions; it's just their approach to life."

Today, it's imperative that all of us have a system to keep ourselves apprised of broader currents. If you actively track the trends, you bring more to the table. You can better help your company wrestle with technological, demographic, social, regulatory, lifestyle, and global trends. By delving more deeply into your industry, you make yourself the resident expert, which doesn't exactly hurt your chances of career advancement either.

Here are three components to developing your own future-scan system:

Component 1: Make Time for Reading   Many executives barely have time to flip through the *Wall Street Journal* and the weekly business magazines, much less keep up with general interest publications. After a grueling day, they want something escapist and entertaining.

Lack of good reading habits can hurt you. An effective personal future-scan system must include broad-based reading of high-quality material. Subscribe to a variety of publications, even if you aren't able to read them all immediately. Then when you're on a flight or have a block of unscheduled free time, whittle away at the stack. Even if you only skim them, you'll pick up a wealth of information and you'll notice connections and start seeing patterns of change emerge. In addition:

- *Take stock of your reading diet.* What newspapers, magazines, newsletters, e-zines, and trade publications do you read? Is your information diet broad enough?

- *Read widely.* Pick up a copy of *Seventeen* or *People* or *Chain Store Age* or *Fast Company* (the voice of the Innovation Movement). Look for what's different, incongruous, worrisome, exciting. Professional trend forecasters call this "scanning and monitoring." The goal is to notice and to read what jumps out at you. When you spot something unusual, ask yourself: How might this trend become an opportunity?

- *Read for different points of view.* Accept free literature and sample issue offers. You never know where a new idea may come from. Buckminster Fuller supposedly bought the top right-hand magazine whenever he visited a newsstand, no matter what magazine it was. One such purchase was a science magazine that contained an article about the eye of a housefly. It is said that this article inspired him to invent the geodesic dome.

- *Read up on at least one new subject every week.* It might be a new technological or scientific breakthrough or emerging political or social issue. Make it a point to read in-depth articles on the subject, even if you aren't particularly interested. The more you understand about the other pieces of the puzzle, the less likely something will blindside you.

- *Scan your mail.* Even your junk mail, including e-mail, can convey patterns of change. Scan conference brochures and advertisements for clues. For example, the Comdex program, which is mailed to thousands of prospective attendees every year, offers a particularly concise window on the technology world, and monitoring conference brochures from other industries can alert you to trends and issues you might otherwise miss.

- *File hard copies to store the information you save.* There's power in being able to lay your hands on an article, report, or seminar handout when you need it. Highlight excerpts with special meaning and significance to you. Post-it Notes and highlight markers can remind you of the value you first saw in the material that you may want to quote later in speeches or memos and reports.

The bottom line is this: Leaders are readers. Take stock of your reading habits and keep working to improve the quality and variety of what you read.

Component 2: Connect with People   The people in your life have a tremendous influence on how you think, on what you think about, and on your ability to spot opportunities in change.

To connect with people, join networking groups and professional and trade associations; attend special focus conferences. Ask questions. Do those in your present circle of contacts challenge you to think new thoughts, to grow, indeed, to assault your assumptions? Or do they merely reinforce attitudes, knowledge, and perspectives you already hold? "Better a nettle in my side than my echo," wrote the 17th century transcendentalist Ralph Waldo Emerson in an essay on friendship. Those who unflinchingly bring differences of opinion to us may not always echo back to us what we want to hear. But what they will do is make us more effective in a world of change.

Component 3: Observe Yourself   The greatest opportunity-spotters are not only good readers and networkers, they are also self-observant. They listen to their intuition, that little voice inside that says, "wait a minute, this is important." Or "this doesn't feel right," or "I don't think our customers will want this."

Fred Smith, chairman of FedEx, told me in a 1985 interview that most people have an inherent resistance to what he called "kaleidoscope thinking." "They tend to judge the future as an extrapolation of the past. Maybe it's more comfortable that way. But if you want to innovate, you have to be capable of making intuitive judgments. Most people who innovate have this enormous thirst for information. What they're trying to do is hedge their bets. Really, intuition is not so much intuition as the amalgamation of a lot of stuff from a lot of different places, which leads you to say, 'okay, it's a safe bet. It's not a fool's bet.'"

Imagine yourself as a customer of your company. Then ask, "What might I want that isn't available? What do I like? What are my own needs that are not being filled by this company and its product and services?"

Reading, interacting with people, and taking the time to develop your own perspective on events and trends are ways to add value to yourself and to better contribute to your firm's future.

Mining Strategy 3:
Integrate Future Scanning with Your Idea Management System

Companies often establish a future-scan group only after there has been a major oversight, a missed opportunity, or an unpleasant surprise. While better late than never, this behavior seldom unleashes the imaginative dialogue needed to seize the future. Innovation Vanguard companies, on the other hand, proactively upgrade their scanning processes not just to avert disaster, but to get a jump on opportunities.

BMW Group's Future Scan System   In 1997, Munich, Germany-based Bavarian Motor Works (BMW) felt it necessary to rethink and redesign its methods of mining the future. Being the "ultimate driving machine" is a tall order, given the technological and competitive clockspeed in the auto industry and the need to differentiate itself at the premium end of the market. The firm thus organized a Central Innovation Organization in Munich, composed of 35 people to coordinate its efforts. This group in turn manages six innovation "fields," 100-person, widely dispersed networks of BMW managers and engineers that focus on such issues as comfort and convenience, safety and security, and environmental or what it calls "green" issues. Each field is responsible for early identification and reporting on new developments, trends, regulatory changes, and of course emerging technologies.

To support the field's work, the firm also established a number of satellite outposts in places ranging from Tokyo to Los Angeles to Palo Alto to provide a local listening presence.

The Palo Alto, California, outpost facility is typical. BMW's offices have no sign outside, and the visitor is led into an open, airy facility lined with car body and chassis parts, and engineers working at computers or engaged in passionate discussions. A 20-person group is charged with imagining how emerging technologies might be applied to future automobiles, giving BMW first-mover advantage. The staff scans technology publications and monitors developments in nearby Silicon Valley, attending technology fairs, electronics conferences, and networking events.

The group does more than engage in "blue sky" thinking. Success is measured by how well the team not only discovers interesting technologies, but also by how many technologies it can get adopted into future automobile designs. In the basement of the Palo Alto facility, a parking garage has been converted into a makeshift proto-typing center, and BMW autos are retrofitted with all sorts of exper-imental gadgets. Periodically the garage doors fly open and swarms of BMWs go out in convoys to test-drive on California's freeways.

If a new application is deemed feasible, the Palo Alto group must then use its selling skills to persuade one of the six councils to adopt its idea. To break down the "not invented here" barrier that so stymied Xerox's PARC, BMW rotates engineers from the firm's main design center in Munich through stints in Palo Alto, and the hope is that returnees become champions for the new application once back at Munich headquarters.

Your Future-Scan System Must Fit Your Company   Future scanning doesn't have to be as elaborate as BMW's. A distribution firm uses a simple 10-person cross-functional team to read general interest mag-azines, technology publications, trade magazines, and newsletters. These range from highly technical publications to popular periodi-cals such as *Business 2.0, Fast Company, Wired, Fortune,* and *Investors Business Daily.* Each participant is asked to clip material that might have potential impact on the company: advertisements, articles, edi-torials, etc. In quarterly meetings, participants are asked to comment briefly on what hit them about the information when they first read it and why.

Organizing an opportunity-scanning process is an effective way to take some of the fuzz out of the front end of the innovation process. Think tank participants should represent people from vari-ous functional areas, should include maverick personality types, and should be voluntary. This is integral to making innovation a disci-pline and as such doesn't supplant the traditional strategic planning process. Instead, it takes away that department's monopoly status and embeds the organization with an alternate, systematic way of mining the future.

The important thing is to build awareness, to lay the groundwork for ideation, and to stimulate new thinking.

Mining Strategy 4:
Assault Industry Assumptions

Assumptions are what "everybody knows to be true" but may no longer be. Today assumptions often get obsoleted by reality before we have let go of them. Too often, strategic planning consists of tired assumptions merely being projected forward without any real thought. Too often companies are stymied by narrow or rigid assumptions about how fast they can grow, what markets they might serve, and what existing customers will expect tomorrow. Mining the future, then, has a lot to do with identifying assumptions that can hold us back.

How to assault assumptions? First, by recognizing that this is part of the discipline of innovation. Regis McKenna is a pioneer in the field of public relations who helped Apple Computer, Genentech, and other startups gain credibility. McKenna, chairman of McKenna Group, told us about a rule in his company, which provides strategy consulting to technology firms: If you're going to hold a meeting, everyone must come with a list of questions to stimulate an assumption-assaulting discussion.

Similarly, the late Sam Walton encouraged questions as he built Wal-Mart into the world's largest corporation. "Our company works best when we continue to ask questions," says Maxie Carpenter, vice president of personnel and training for Wal-Mart's Supercenter division. Wal-Mart encourages questions in many ways, from store visits and conference calls to focus groups and grassroots meetings at headquarters with store managers.

Questioning why management does things the way it does isn't always comfortable. It must be encouraged, sanctioned, and modeled by leadership as part of the company's culture. It must be unimpeded by rank or politics. This is easy to say, difficult to do. Things that should be said aren't. As an outside facilitator, speaker, and consultant to numerous organizations each year, I've had more than a few hosts tell me during a preparatory conversation, "Now, you probably don't want to mention x or y or z because the folks are a little sensitive." My response is always "as you wish," but I try to encourage a free-ranging discussion that leaves all issues and trends on the table.

Mining Strategy 5:
Broaden Your Company's Vision

No doubt your firm has a vision statement. Ironically, instead of inspiring vision, it could limit it. Consider:

- If Disney defined its vision as theme parks and animated motion pictures, it would never have moved into hotels, Broadway shows, retail stores, cruise ships, and a myriad of other businesses.

- If Microsoft defined its vision as software, it never would have diversified into the 1001 businesses it is now into, from travel to encyclopedias, real estate to automobile sales.

- If Kimberly-Clark had limited its vision to existing product categories, it might not have "invented" whole new products (disposable training pants, adult diapers, etc.).

- If GE had defined itself as a manufacturer, it would not have envisioned its future in services, and GE Capital would not be the growth engine it represents today.

What about your firm? When was the last time you looked at how you define your industry with an eye toward broadening that definition? Yours may be a manufacturing company today, but might your future be in service as well?

Embracing Growth at GE   Lewis L. Edelheit, Ph.D., GE's senior vice president for Corporate Research and Development and director of GE's Research and Development Center in Schenectady, New York, is a big believer in the power of broadening your firm's vision of itself in order to embrace future growth opportunities. Until a few years ago, Edelheit explained in an article, GE's businesses were structured as a pyramid, with the base as the product and the other elements—services, manufacturing processes and information—built upon that base.

"We have literally turned the pyramid upside down to where the product becomes just one piece of the picture, the tip of that inverted pyramid," writes Edelheit. "The biggest growth opportunities might come from providing services to the customer: providing the customer with ways to become more productive and with information so valuable the customer will pay for it."

Mining Strategy 6:
Strategize Your Place in the First Mover, Fast Follower Race

Much has been written in recent years about "first mover" advantages—the rewards and benefits of being first to discover and commercialize a new product, service, technology, process, or business model. For many observers it is a deeply held assumption that such market pioneers enjoy enduring advantages. During the height of the late 1990s dot-com bubble, such thinking reached the level of a self-evident truth.

Academic research strongly supported this assumption. One study, for example, purported to show that of 25 market pioneers in 1923, 19 were still market leaders today, and that all 25 were still in the top five in their respective categories. Another study, based on analyzing the U.S. government-sponsored Profit Impact of Market Strategies (PIMS) database, concluded that more than 70 percent of current category leaders had been the market pioneers.

Then came the revisionists, the assumption assaulters as it were. Researchers Gerard Tellis and Peter Golder hypothesized that the research cited above and other studies may have been skewed because it looked only at *surviving* firms—those likely to promote themselves as first movers, whether they really were or not. In conducting their research, Tellis and Golder relied instead on analysis of news articles and annual reports written about the companies at the time the product was launched. They supplemented this analysis with interviews with company insiders at the time the market was developing and analysis of reports written when the markets were still in their infancy, to form a different picture.

After studying 50 product categories from their inception, the two reported in *Sloan Management Review* that self-described pioneers (defined as "the first to sell in a new product category") were market-share leaders today in *only 4 out of 50 product categories*. Their conclusion: the failure rate of market pioneers of 47 percent is higher for durables than nondurables, and market pioneers are still market leaders in only 11 percent of the categories. Calling your firm a first mover, conclude Tellis and Golder, doesn't mean you really were.

- While Procter & Gamble's Pampers unit might boast that it "literally created the disposable diaper business in the United States,"

Tellis and Golder found that disposable diapers were available as early as 1935 from Chux brand of Chicopee, Wisconsin.

- Apple Computer might be remembered as having pioneered the personal computer industry, but that distinction actually goes to Micro Instrumentation and Telemetry Systems—MITS—not exactly a household brand today.

- Miller Lite, which Miller Brewing claims was the first low-calorie beer, was preceded by Rheingold Brewery's Gablinger Light, launched a full decade before.

Do Tellis and Golder's findings mean that companies should never attempt to be first to sell in a new product or service category, or to pioneer new business models? Not at all. What their findings do mean is that mining your firm's future means constantly attempting to be first in *discovering* new opportunities but not necessarily that you *move first to develop the market, product, or strategic opportunity*. Because of Tellis and Golder's work as well as a growing volume of research of the world's best thinkers in the area of "innovation timing advantages," you can avoid the mistakes other companies have made. More importantly, you and your firm can benefit from the practices that brought some first movers tremendous growth, breakthrough product success, and commensurate profits.

Before Pioneering, Consider These Questions   You can earn the title first mover with that new idea you're considering but will it benefit your top and bottom line? Will it create the growth you seek? The time to consider such issues is before proceeding blindly down a path lined with rosy scenarios and unchallenged assumptions.

Lasting benefits accrue to firms that can honestly answer yes to these seven questions:

1. ***Do you have proprietary technology or designs that can be protected by patents, copyrights, or other means?***

If you have scientific know-how that your competitors don't (and can't readily acquire), you might have the potential to break out a product or service that gives you a significant, sustainable market edge. Pharmaceutical companies have exploited the legal protection afforded to their industry for years (drugs are protected for 12 years by patents), and a similar situation exists with medical tech devices, at least in theory. Count on having to defend your patents though, from imitators.

2. Can you, by going first, preempt assets or investment capital from going to competitors?

Many dot-com firms in the late 1990s came to market with essentially the same idea at the same time. But the initial edge often went to the first one or ones to secure large amounts of venture capital, essentially preempting investment capital from going to others who came along later with the same idea. (At least until the dot-com crash of 2000, when whole categories were obliterated because their business models failed to explain an even more fundamental question: How does this idea deliver value to real customers?)

Assets aren't confined to capital by any means. If you have physical assets such as supermarket shelf space or valuable territory such as a desirable location, these could also afford you a sustainable first-mover advantage.

3. Can you achieve brand loyalty by going first?

If first movers can make a big enough splash fast enough, they can establish a reputation for being the best, most trusted brand. Brand loyalty in effect preempts demand, instead of preempting assets or supply. Although not a first mover in the market for word-processing software, Microsoft Word was the first word-processing software to be adopted by millions of customers. For them, switching to an alternate brand would require learning a new program. Often, as we'll explore in a later chapter, that's more trouble than it's worth, so customers become loyal to a product even though they find it less than satisfying.

4. Can you enhance your reputation by going first?

There's no question that being the first mover can endear a product or brand to customers. In the minds of consumers, brands such as Kleenex, Post-it Notes, and Walkman are synonymous with the product and the product category. That, in a nutshell, is the benefit of having what scholars in this area of innovation call "reputation effects."

Theoretically, anyone can copy the "look and feel" of a service sector innovation, whether Starbucks, California Pizza Kitchen, Hard Rock Café, or Disneyland. Only actual logos and trademarks can be protected. These and other first movers enjoy reputational effects because they went first and had a superior or unique offering. Later entrants wind up being perceived as ho-hum also-rans or worse, copycats.

On the other hand, if you rely on the supposed strength of your brand or your reputation, yet fail to deliver better value, you can lose the market to competitors. Sony was also first to market with its BETA version of the videocassette recorder (VCR), well before other consumer electronics manufacturers even had such a product in the planning stages. Yet Sony shot itself in the foot by trying to keep BETA proprietary and was overtaken by later VCRs that relied on VHS technology, leaving Sony with a shrinking, moribund market that eventually the company was forced to abandon altogether.

5. Do you have a vision of the mass market?

To receive first-mover payoff, you must continually assault your assumptions about the market potential of your idea. If you don't, somebody else will.

In pioneering the disposable diaper market, first mover Chux limited itself to targeting wealthy households and marketed its diaper for "special circumstances," such as car trips. But second mover Procter & Gamble had a vision of a much bigger mass market, where moms and dads would use disposables all the time instead of then-common cloth diapers. P&G used its expertise in consumer research to improve Pampers, and its marketing muscle and distribution reach to make Pampers a growth engine for decades.

In 1979, AT&T commissioned a market research study to size up the market for its new invention: the cellular phone. The study predicted a subscriber base of only 800,000 by year 2000, concluding there was "no market at any price." AT&T stayed out of the business, leaving it to local phone companies and independent operators to pursue. For a time, it appeared the forecast was right. Cellular service was unreliable and expensive (handsets cost thousands of dollars), installation was cumbersome and available only in cars. Sales volume wasn't enough to offset the large infrastructure costs, and cellular companies suffered huge losses.

But all that changed when leading cellular companies envisioned a mass market for their service and took action. McCaw Cellular bought up local providers, worked with manufacturing partners to reduce the cost and size of handsets, broadened its target market beyond an elite group of executives, and offered below-cost handsets with service contracts. Result: McCaw achieved annual growth rates of 40 percent to 50 percent for years. By 2000, there were over 80 million cellular subscribers in the United States alone, 100 times as many as the initial study had predicted. Instead of owning the market, AT&T had to buy its way into the market, acquiring McCaw for $11.5 billion in 1994.

6. Is your management team willing to be persistent over time?

Breakthrough inventions sometimes catch fire with customers right away, as the Internet and the World Wide Web did during the years 1995 to 2000. The same is sometimes true for breakthrough innovations, those that move your firm's growth needle almost immediately after you launch them. Witness the Chrysler Minivan, Gillette's Sensor, Disneyland, DirecTV, and numerous other examples.

Other times, however, breakthrough products and new business models are the fruit of dozens upon dozens of small, incremental improvements in design, manufacturing, and market building over a period of years that finally qualify them as breakthroughs. Sometimes, a long period of often slow progress in research and development precedes the launch, after which a period of long and often slow post-launch market-building activity is necessary to convert customers to the new idea and begin to show a profit. DuPont's Kevlar, as we'll explore more fully in a later chapter, took years of market building activity to become a bona-fide breakthrough product for that company.

During both phases of what we've defined earlier as radical innovations, you must be persistent, especially if it represents a radically new way to solve the customer's problem. Persistence is required through the comings and goings of CEOs, boards of directors, innovation champions, and so on.

RCA pioneered color television in 1954, yet sales lagged for years because the vast majority of programs were broadcast in black and white. RCA's long-term persistence in building color technology ensured acceptance. It accomplished this goal two ways: First, a program of technical research led to improvements in quality and protected those improvements with patents the company licensed profitably for years. Second, a commitment to broadcasting color television programs through its NBC subsidiary gradually built demand for color.

The message is clear: If you and your firm have short-shrifted projects with a longer-term time horizon, this isn't the place to start in trying to change your culture. Persistence, in individuals or on the part of management teams, is never easy to instill if it has long been lacking. All too often, projects start out with lots of enthusiasm and adequate financing, only to be shortchanged the minute the political winds change, profits soften, or a new CEO comes to the helm.

In 1967, Rheingold Brewery spent $5.5 million to build market share for its Gablinger Light beer in the eastern United States. Unfortunately, sales of its regular beer fell that year and in response, the company's directors fired top management in favor of more profit-conscious leaders. The new management dropped support for Gablinger's Light and the product died.

Compare Rheingold's response with second mover Miller Lite's introduction. In 1975, *Business Week* reported that Lite's advertising expenditures averaged $6.50 per barrel, while the industry average was only $1. Further, Philip Morris, Miller's parent, was willing to forgo profits from all Miller brands for five years in order to build market share and establish the light beer category. Miller's financial commitment was rewarded by long-term leadership in light beer, even after a swarm of imitators jumped into the market.

7. Are you willing & able to relentlessly keep on innovating after you've launched the idea?

Long-term leadership requires continuous post-launch improvements. Unfortunately, internal considerations often hinder companies from investing in and following through on good ideas. They might fear cannibalizing established products as IBM did, when it stymied development of minicomputers and workstations to protect mainframe sales, even as competitors were making inroads into the mainframe market.

Ampex's failure to bring video recorders to the home market was caused partly by management's satisfaction with sales to the professional market. In company cultures that are bureaucratic and factionalized, this needed post-launch aggressiveness is slowed or stopped when second movers appear on the scene. Sustained leadership requires a solid commitment not only to build a bigger pie, but a relentless drive for value-adding improvements that continue to drive growth.

Unless you are strategic in your approach to the front end of innovation, and carefully work through these questions, "fast followers" will likely steal your thunder. Larger firms with substantial resources sometimes benefit by waiting for the resolution of uncertainties and to see if customers perceive value in the first mover's idea. Others can sometimes buy up the first mover's product or service or company, as we saw with AT&T's purchase of McCaw.

These second movers can benchmark and copy what works; they don't have to speculate. They can ask users and existing customers for suggestions on improving the first mover's product.

Designing Your 21st Century Future-Mining Capability

For the customer, the ultimate issue is not which product got to market first or which company came out with the new business model before the others. What customers care most about is which company or product or service wins their loyalty by providing not only the new way to solve their problem or satisfy their need, but the best total solution overall, the best value of doing so.

To gain growth by going first, you must carefully study the individual situation, the cultural barriers inside your firm, the resources available, the conditions in your industry and in the individual marketplace before strategizing a course of action. It's best to think of all important innovation projects from the largest possible context and to, as Steven Covey has it, "begin with the end in mind." Otherwise you might end up doing the pioneering work of designing and building the product or service and even go about the arduous task of building a new market, only to find fast-following competitors come along and eat your lunch.

When it comes to mining the future, there's little question that innovation-adept firms do things differently. Here's a quick recap of the important ideas in this chapter that you can use to make the front end less fuzzy and more productive.

1. How satisfied are you that the way you personally scan and monitor trends is adequate to give you an edge in spotting threats, and identifying opportunities?

2. How effective and systematic is your firm's future-scan system, and what steps might you take to strengthen this system?

3. How integrated is your current future-mining capability with your firm's idea management system?

4. Do you and your firm regularly seek to assault your industry's assumptions, and broaden the vision of where your firm might seek opportunity in the future?

5. How systematic are you in strategically thinking through and developing a longer-range plan for each new product, service, and market that you pursue?

With concerted attention to the front end of innovation, you'll soon be ready to take on the next stage of designing a 21st century innovation strategy. You'll be ready to fortify your firm's idea factory, which is the subject of our next chapter.

CHAPTER 6

Fortifying the Idea Factory

Innovation isn't just a front-end activity;
we need creative solutions all along the process.
—Nancy Eicher
Director of Innovation, Pillsbury Unit of General Mills

In the mid-1990s a group of professors at New York's Rensselaer Polytechnic Institute were gathered around the coffee urn one day when one of them had a harebrained idea. Wouldn't it be interesting to be a fly on the wall inside some of these large corporations and observe how they go about the process of coming up with ideas?

This team didn't just shrug off the comment and return to the lecture halls. They received funding from the Institute of Industrial Research in Washington, D.C. and carried out an unusual study, publishing their findings in numerous journals and an important book. The researchers were granted "real time" access to key people working on radical ideas the companies themselves deemed highly promising. They returned every few months for updates on such projects as GE's digital X-ray, Texas Instruments' digital light projector, GM's hybrid vehicle, IBM's silicon-germanium devices, DuPont's biodegradable polymer, and Otis' bidirectional elevator. In all, the team studied 12 projects inside 10 companies.

Where did the ideas come from? Think "happy accident" and you pretty much get the picture.

- In 4 of the 12 projects, the idea came from individuals or small groups working on their own initiative—"freelancing"—rather than being directed by a new venture board or other idea management system.

- GM's hybrid vehicle project came about as the result of a casual conversation.

- Two Analog Devices engineers visited a customer's manufacturing facility and used the occasion to inquire about possible applications for a particular unmarketed technology they had developed. This chance encounter triggered a possible solution to an industry "holy grail," a problem everybody in the industry believes is impossible to solve. Unfortunately, noted the Rensselaer team, this company's scanning activity ceased with retirement of the two engineers.

- In 5 of the 12 projects, an impending threat to the company's core business or a period of slowed growth generated a desperate call from senior management for new ideas.

Happenstance? You bet. Ad hoc? No question. Seat of the pants? Absolutely. "Almost without exception," the team concluded, "these idea-generation methods have been applied sporadically, rather than systematically, continuously and strategically. In no case [we know of] has an on-going process been set up that regularly requests such ideas. *What we observed were one-time acts, or new systems put in place whose staying power remains unproven.*"

Is it any wonder with this kind of fuzziness at the front end, the eventual products either bombed or were never commercialized? Otis' bi-directional elevator, which would enable construction of mile-high buildings was dead on arrival when launched in 1999; the company never sold a single one. GM's hybrid vehicle has yet to be launched, while hybrid models from Toyota and Honda have become breakthrough products.

Fortifying the Idea Factory

1. Involve everyone in the quest for ideas.

2. Involve customers in your ideation process.

3. Involve customers in new ways.

4. Focus on the unarticulated needs of customers.

5. Seek ideas from new customer groups.

6. Involve suppliers in product ideation.

7. Benchmark ideation methods.

How Innovation Vanguard Companies Are Rethinking Ideation

Inventing the future will always have an element of serendipity to it. Breakthroughs can never be commanded from the top, nor churned out on deadline. Is it any wonder the 75 percent of companies that are consistently disappointed with their innovation abilities have trouble filling the pipeline with promising new products, services, process improvements, and strategic initiatives? In sharp contrast, the other 25 percent—the Innovation Vanguard—are continuously reinventing and refining and giving attention to fortifying their idea factories. They recognize the simple reality: If good ideas don't get hatched, they surely aren't going to get launched down the line.

The Innovation Vanguard firms make a concerted effort to cultivate conditions where happy accidents are more likely to occur. They are reinventing ideation so that greater numbers of ideas funnel into their pipelines and advance via their idea management processes toward implementation.

Ideation is the systematic process of looking for ideas using state of the art techniques. The goal is the formation or conception of ideas, which are the building blocks of new products, services, processes, and strategies. This chapter examines the seven strategies listed in the box above for fortifying the idea factory at your firm.

Ideation Strategy 1:
Involve Everyone in the Quest for Ideas

In Chapter 4, "Empowering the Idea Management Process," we observed that the consensus among Innovation Vanguard firms was that suggestion systems that ask employees for their ideas are passé. Why? Because they limit the type of ideas asked for and reward only process ideas: those that save the company money. But then along comes a Vanguard firm with an ideation method that borrows from the suggestion system model to invigorate its quest for ideas.

Ideation at Bristol-Myers Squibb   Bristol-Myers Squibb (BMS) is a New York City-based $21 billion global pharmaceutical firm. While you might think all the ideational action in such a company would be around finding the next breakthrough drug, BMS sees the need for ideas much more broadly.

Marsha MacArthur, grandniece of the late World War II American general Douglas MacArthur, has what is arguably the most unusual job at any drug company in the world: idea searcher. MacArthur works full time designing ideation campaigns for internal customers in the pharmaceutical division. Got a vexing problem? See Marsha, and she'll come to the rescue.

The idea of having these targeted idea catalyst campaigns originated with her boss, Mark Wright, vice president of U.S. market research and business intelligence. MacArthur gets calls from "sponsors," usually project managers looking for new approaches to the business issues they face, which can range widely. When the patent on the firm's breakthrough drug Glucophage was about to expire, the team, with MacArthur's assistance, launched a campaign to solicit ideas internally on how to get more people to use the drug in the interim.

At lunchtime, to publicize the campaign, employees walked around wearing sandwich boards declaring, "we're waging war on diabetes and we need your help" and asking for ideas. Town Hall meetings were held in which the team's problem was outlined in greater detail. How do we drive patients into doctors' offices? How do we get patients to convert from the diabetes drug they are now using to try ours? Employees were directed to submit any ideas they had on how to rev up sales of Glucophage to BMS's intranet site, where tips on submitting their ideas could be found. One suggestion: run a national campaign and declare war on diabetes. Another was for a museum for diabetics.

"I was really proud of everybody and the ideas that were submitted," says MacArthur. "There weren't obvious ones like, 'talk to doctors;' hey, we already do that. They were quite well thought out." In all, that particular campaign generated 4000 inquiries, and 429 employees thought enough of their ideas to type them up and submit them, a 7-percent submission rate.

Employees based as far away as Poland submitted ideas to the division's headquarters in Plainsboro, New Jersey. A specially formed team of evaluators sifted through all the ideas, selected the top 40, and eventually launched the Be Aggressive Campaign. All submitters received letters thanking them, and certificates and prizes were awarded in some cases. In a typical year, MacArthur will conduct 20 to 30 campaigns for sponsors who approach her; some will be in her division, others will be enterprise-wide. With each campaign, she carefully targets, using sophisticated idea management software, different sectors of the employee base, so as not to overwhelm people.

How to Involve Everyone   A big part of making ideation an enterprise-wide responsibility involves making sure the voice of the customer pervades every part of your organization, not just certain departments like sales, marketing, or service. Bring customers into your firm and into your process at every opportunity. Provide the means for your people to get out in the field or on the telephones listening to everyday customers and observe everyday service interactions.

In recent years, some companies have taken steps to enlarge the number of employees involved in new product/service ideation. Unless participants are involved in listening to customers though, you may be wasting your time. Don't allow any manager, technical specialist, purchasing, finance, or human resource professional to participate in product, service, or market development decisions unless they're spending at least 20 percent of their time with current or prospective customers and suppliers.

Ideation Strategy 2:
Involve Customers in Your Process

Where do most product ideas come from? In their study of 252 new products at 123 firms, researchers Kleinschmidt and Cooper report that new products are most often initiated by ideas from customers, rather than from in-house brainstorming sessions or developed internally by research and development.

Involving customers in your company's ideation process can be accomplished in a number of ways. You can form an advisory board of key customers to serve as a sounding board. You can identify those who show a pattern of purchasing new versions of your products first. While their ideas must be validated with probes of the overall market, these "lead adoptors" can provide you with advanced insights into where the market is headed and how you might best respond.

Most customer-driven ideation methods are rooted in traditional market research techniques ranging from focus groups to quantitative and qualitative surveys. Such methods help uncover unexploited opportunities and dissatisfaction with current offerings that could allow competitor inroads. The limitation of such methods in most industries has to do with the fact that your competitors are asking the same people these same questions. Result: little in the way of creativity, and more of the same. But Innovation Vanguard companies are doing things differently.

BMW's Dialogue with Customers   Munich-based BMW is constantly seeking to discover new technologies and design features to put into future cars. Its interest is not limited to internal research groups, or even to the insights gleaned by listening posts in Palo Alto, California, Tokyo, Japan, and other places. It also extends an invitation to ideate to "creative minds outside the BMW Group." To harvest their insights, the firm's Virtual Innovation Agency (VIA, for short) is the point of contact for all external innovators who do not as yet have contacts within the firm. VIA makes it easy for car buffs to communicate their ideas through its website, with additional online discussions that solicit ideas from fans around the world. Within the first week after VIA was launched in July 2001, 4000 ideas had been received. VIA is a highly sophisticated idea submission process that allows anyone with access to the Internet to submit ideas and to have those ideas protected. The suggester is prompted through a process that allows him or her to know what the company is and is not interested in hearing about and to get feedback on whether the idea has potential. If it is, the idea is routed to the appropriate field group for follow-up.

Ideation Strategy 3:
Involve Customers in New Ways

Industries and companies evolve and embrace new methods at different rates. Nowhere is this more evident than in their ways of listening to customers. Methods that are passé to one industry may be state-of-the-art to another. Surveying customers might be old hat in many industries, but for homebuilders, it's relatively new.

Retooling the Idea Factory at KB Home Market-leading homebuilder KB Home, based in Los Angeles, did not begin surveying customers until the late 1990s. Yet the insights they gained since then have led to a whole new way of doing business. In the Denver market, where the company is a major player, KB Home assumed that people wanted fireplaces and basements, so that's what KB Home built. Then one day Bruce Karatz, KB Home's CEO, happened to be visiting one of the firm's model homes there when he overheard what amounted to a high-pressure pitch to a couple of prospective buyers. The buyers were looking to save money; they didn't want a basement. The salesman was pushing the couple to accept it like every other buyer had.

Karatz decided then and there that KB Home would survey customers. The findings have since jackhammered many a preconceived notion about what homebuyers want. In the Denver market, surveys showed many people preferred doing without basements, especially when omitting the basement cut the price of a home by as much as 20 percent. In Phoenix, a covered porch was considered mandatory until surveys revealed that less than half the buyers cared about them. "The preferences were probably there for years," observed Karatz, "but we never bothered to ask."

By polling for preferences, KB Home didn't just eliminate amenities such as porches, fireplaces, and basements to provide budget-conscious buyers a lower overall price. Instead, surveying encouraged the company to offer an array of amenities: coffee bars in the master bedroom, built-in home offices, higher quality windows. Not only did the amenities please buyers, they increased the home's selling price and fueled top-line growth. Amenity customization also created havoc for competitors who were locked into the familiar, one-size-fits-all approach. KB Home found that because it builds so many homes (17,000 in a recent year), the new survey-led approach allows it to hold down prices while offering greater choices that other homebuilders can't match.

KB Home is hardly the only builder now relying on customer surveying. But accepted practices in listening to customers evolve differently in different industries. Who then might be at the leading edge? Automakers. Faced with ferocious global competition and the need to wager billions of dollars for a new line, auto manufacturers are often the "early adoptors" of new ideational techniques.

Using Archetype Research at DaimlerChrysler   Automakers are currently employing ethnography, a branch of anthropology that deals with understanding native cultures. DaimlerChrysler's PT Cruiser, introduced in 2000, was the first vehicle designed using an ideation process known as "archetype research." Chrysler has shifted much of its market-research program over to the method, which was introduced to the firm by French-born medical anthropologist G. Clotaire Rapaille. Working with autistic children may seem far afield from the business of trying to divine what fickle car-buyers will want next, but Rapaille's approach borrows heavily from his training there.

PT Cruiser's development team sought to create a vehicle that mixed retro and futuristic elements to attract a cult following similar to Volkswagen's revamped Beetle or the original Mustang. With Rapaille calling the shots, the design team took an early prototype and hit the road to get customer input at sessions in Europe, South America, Asia, and the United States.

In traditional focus groups, participants are chosen because they fit a particular demographic profile: young men, 18 to 24, say. But participants for these sessions were picked to represent an entire country's culture. Rapaille opened the three-hour sessions by telling participants, seated in a circle near a life-sized PT Cruiser prototype, "I'm from another planet, and I don't even know what you do with that. What's the purpose of that thing?" Participants were given pens and paper and asked to write stories triggered by the prototype.

During the second hour, people were asked to use scissors and a pile of magazines to cut out words and pictures to help them describe their feelings about the prototype they were looking at. During the third hour, visitors were asked to lie on the floor, with the lights dimmed, and soothing music filling the room. The group was told to relax, and they were invited to let their minds drift back to childhood and recall those memories invoked by the prototype.

After each session, the team pored over the stories with yellow highlight markers, sleuthing for the emotion sparked by the vehicle, or what Rapaille calls "the reptilian hot buttons." The insights from this highly unusual approach were nothing short of astonishing. Participants contrasted a dangerous outside world with desire for a secure interior and ultrasafe vehicle. "It's a jungle out there," was a strong theme. At one session, participants revealed that the prototype on display looked insubstantial and unsafe. In another, participants described the vehicle as too "toy-like." The prototype's large rear window, attendees suggested, allowed "prying outsiders" to see in. Participants felt the car would be especially dangerous if hit from behind. The overarching message: "give me a big thing like a tank."

In response, PT Cruiser's fenders were enlarged and given more bulbous curves to give owners a greater feeling of prowess. The rear window was made smaller than designers originally conceived. And after sessions indicated that the initial design "wasn't creative enough," designers came up with a rakish forward-sloping roof that had the additional benefit of creating additional interior space.

Introduced in North America in April 2000, PT Cruiser became an immediate breakthrough product for the firm, and Chrysler has since expanded the use of this unconventional ideation method. Is ethnography the wave of the future or just another fad? Time will tell, but one thing is clear. In the past, designers, engineers, and marketers have created ideas in a vacuum—the vacuum of their own tastes, knowledge, prejudices, and beliefs. The future of customer-driven ideation is developing new and better ways to listen more deeply. Ethnography and other methods get you closer to your customer/buyer, get you into their psyche, and go beyond what people might say to be socially acceptable. Adopting some of these unconventional processes will enable you and your firm to avoid obvious mistakes and turnoffs, and to enhance features that may have been given short shrift.

Ideation Strategy 4:
Focus on the Unarticulated Needs of Customers

To align your products, services, and customer service practices more closely with customers, conventional wisdom says, "assemble a focus group." Listen to your customers for their ideas. This is fine if you want feedback on existing ideas. But it's woefully inadequate if you want to smoke out what innovation scholars call the *unarticulated needs* of customers.

Here, you are really asking people to think about hypothetical products and ideas, what they'd respond to if it were available.

Consider the microwave oven by way of example. Asked why you like your microwave, you might say, "It heats things up more quickly than a conventional oven." And if you were asked: "how do you use your microwave?" chances are you'd respond: "to heat up water for tea" or "to pop popcorn." Maybe you'd say, "to cook an occasional frozen dinner, when I'm really in a hurry."

You would probably not mention that you cook only certain things with your microwave. That you'd never but never try to cook a roast or a steak in your microwave, because you tried that once, and it came out looking gray and unappetizing. You might still *prefer* to cook a great-tasting roast in half the time, yet that *desire* is not something you would volunteer: it is *unarticulated*. Using ideation techniques that probed unarticulated needs, GE in 1999 came up with Advantium™—a speed cooker that cooks roasts, steaks, and lots of other items in half the time as a traditional microwave. The product, which is similar in size to the traditional microwave oven, uses white hot halogen bulbs to brown and cook the meat's outside while utilizing microwaves to cook the meat's insides.

Listening to Customers at Charles Schwab Listen to David S. Pottruck, co-CEO of Charles Schwab, describe how he listens and creatively interprets what customers are trying to say. "First, I ask customers about their experience with services like ours," he says. "Then I try to listen, beyond what they say, for frustrations and dreams. I almost pretend I'm on a hunt to hear what they would say if they had the necessary experience. I love to ask customers to dream. They describe their problem and their ideal world where the problem disappears. It's up to [us] to listen and to create something to overcome those frustrations, disappointments, and objections."

Pottruck uses the example of Schwab branch offices to illustrate the value of selective listening in getting at what is really important to customers. As Schwab has done since its inception, they ask people questions like: How important is having a local branch office? "And people rate it fairly low, seventh or eighth on a customer's typical wish list," Pottruck reports. Conventional wisdom would have it that Schwab should have gone totally virtual, that bricks and mortar local offices are costly and unnecessary. "Yet every time we open a local office, we double the new business we get in that community." If Schwab ideators simply relied upon market research, they might never open another branch office.

Pottruck had a different perspective. He was aware that even as the company was doing 80 percent of its transactions electronically, people were still opening 70 percent of new accounts face-to-face in branch offices. Why would branches still be important? "Well, when you ask people, 'how important is service?' or 'what are your biggest frustrations?' they'll tell you about websites that are confusing or don't work, or about dealing with people over an 800 number. They'll talk about their fear of having a problem and nobody to resolve it. In many ways the customer doesn't even understand, the local office becomes a security blanket to obviate these concerns. They can't or won't articulate these needs, and the words *branch office* don't trigger the response . . . . Nonetheless, that local human presence is important to many people. If we listened only to the words, we would never open local offices. It's when we listen to fears and frustrations that the need becomes obvious." Pottruck concludes that "sometimes intuition has to override the conclusion of the data."

How Innovators at Callaway Golf Discovered Bertha In the early 1990s, golf clubs looked almost identical. One manufacturer would make a slight incremental improvement and the others would quickly follow. One introduced a new metal or a new grip or otherwise altered the design, and the others played catch-up.

But when Callaway Golf Company launched Big Bertha in 1991, it did not focus on competitors. Callaway's developers went out to country clubs and public courses and hung around. They observed how golfers approached the game and asked how they felt about their level of skill. They talked to former golfers who hadn't set foot on a course in years. They concluded that many people liked the game but didn't play because it was too frustrating.

Callaway's innovation team saw that people wanted to play but were intimidated. So they made a driver with a larger clubhead, which featured an enlarged and more forgiving "sweet spot." They extended the shaft by several inches, which meant the ball would travel farther. They marketed it is as a way to make golf less difficult and more fun. The result was that new players took up the sport and a lot of the seasoned players traded in their old drivers for Berthas as well. Callaway's band of maverick thinkers knew that the low-lying fruit of incremental improvement had been picked already. By focusing on unarticulated needs, they created a blockbuster.

Ideation Strategy 5:
Seek Ideas from New Customer Groups

Chances are, there's a group of people out there you consider to be your customers. If you enlarge the definition of who your customers are, you might just enlarge your ability to spawn winning ideas in the process. What about companies or people who've never done business with you before? What about former customers? What about your competition's customers? And what about your customers' customers?

Listening to Nontraditional Customers at Phillips Electronics The medical products division of Holland-based Phillips asked itself a fundamental question, "Who is our customer?" Before, product managers at the firm had considered only doctors in hospitals to be their customers, since doctors made decisions about suppliers.

But managers began to look more deeply into the changes occurring within the health care industry. In so doing, they noticed that health care service was increasingly being delivered in nontraditional environments: the home, outpatient clinics, even on the street to homeless people. What were the needs of these nontraditional customers?

Phillips soon discovered that one problem these customers were having was hearing inside their patients' bodies. "Hearing heart murmurs or detecting breathing problems with traditional stethoscopes was becoming increasingly difficult, because of all the noise in these nontraditional environments," explains Jay Mazelsky, a general manager at Phillips' Healthcare Solutions Group in Andover, Massachusetts. These people weren't asking for an improved stethoscope that would increase their ability to hear above the din of traffic and voices—*it was an unarticulated need.* Busy making the rounds, these caregivers merely made do with a tool that hadn't changed much in 100 years.

By asking themselves about the needs of these other customer groups, Mazelsky's team was jarred into realizing an opportunity: create a diagnostic tool for nontraditional customers. Phillips and its ideation consultant, IdeaScope Associates, developed the Electronic Stethoscope, which blocks out background noises, such as traffic or voices, and offers 14 times more amplification than a traditional stethoscope. One doctor who used the product noted that she could hear her own heart murmur for the first time.

Since its introduction in 1998, annual sales of the stethoscope have exceeded those of traditional, acoustic models. And the success of the product has spurred the company to think about other needs of nontraditional customers as well.

Ideation Strategy 6:
Involve Suppliers in Product Ideation

How many good ideas have you gotten from your suppliers of late? If not very many, perhaps you aren't asking the right questions. Or establishing the basis for partnering to thrive. The usual stumbling blocks to partnering include a reluctance to share information with vendors, lack of trust, complacency in existing supplier-manufacturer relationships, lack of cooperation between departments within a company, an inability to conceptualize where new opportunities might exist, lack of resources and control systems, and cultural differences. Any or all of these stumbling blocks can mean that "deep partnering" doesn't occur. And in the vast majority of supplier-manufacturer relationships it doesn't, according to an A.T. Kearney survey of 600 global senior executives.

A global purchasing chief at a leading consumer products company used to visit his suppliers from time to time and would always end the visit with a request: "If you have any new ideas or technologies you think we'd be interested in, be sure to let us know." And his suppliers would always say, "you'll be the first person we'll call." They never did.

This purchaser now involves suppliers in the ideation process. He begins the conversation by saying, "You know, I think in the past I've been a bad customer. I didn't tell you what I needed, I only told you what I wanted. What I need is to know is, for example, whether you might have an adhesive that would work well on elderly skin, sensitive skin, bruised skin, diseased skin, and five other kinds of skin that we've identified." By articulating its unsolved problems, he and his team have made a big difference in encouraging suppliers to contribute to the company's ideation process. This process moves procurement from doing the merely routine tasks to adding value to departments ranging from R&D to marketing.

The new approach has been much more productive in aiding ideation: "Even one of our notoriously noncreative suppliers developed two proprietary materials for the company in the last 12 months. It's unbelievable how excited some of our suppliers get when we ask them to be creative in our behalf."

These firms cultivate relationships with vendors using four simple guidelines:

- *You must share the risks as well as the rewards.*
  What are the risks for a supplier in investing time and resources in your new product if it fails in the marketplace? If the supplier puts its smartest R&D people on your project and it bombs, the supplier has no way to amortize the costs of that investment with orders in the future.

- *You must share information with key suppliers.*
  Suppliers who have earned your trust should be involved in early design stage ideation. Hold ongoing focus groups with them to solicit their feedback. The sooner you can share information about new product plans, and the sooner you solicit feedback from key suppliers on your prototypes, the sharper your market edge.

- *You must engage in mutual measurement.*
  Establish a method by which you and your supplier both measure the effectiveness of the relationship. As with any marriage,

the supplier and manufacturer must work on the relationship. Motorola's Supplier Advisory Council is composed of Motorola officials plus 15 top suppliers who rotate on and off over time. The council deals with policy level issues, such as which suppliers will supply which materials to Motorola at what prices, and gives Motorola the opportunity to gain feedback about what's working and what's not from the suppliers' standpoint.

- ***You must encourage teamwork and cooperation.***
  Move from a traditional adversarial relationship characterized by competition between suppliers to one of cooperation encouraged by the buyer organization. Rather than making demands, actively solicit ideas and suggestions.

Ideation Strategy 7:
Benchmark Ideation Methods

Every company works with ideas, but innovation-adept companies actively organize ongoing ideation. The difference is more than semantics. Few companies look at how and where they ideate from the standpoint of how this vital part of the ideas-to-results process might be improved. Few examine the climate in which ideation takes place in their firms. And even fewer ask who is in charge of making this process better, more productive, and more "out of the box."

Our conclusion, based on examining Innovation Vanguard firms, is that this is not something to be left to chance. You need ideation specialists who can be called on to teach new techniques, to shake things up, inject maverick-thinking, and raise awareness. One is the old brainstorming no-no of mixing ideation, which is coming up with ideas, with analysis, which begins to happen the moment somebody in a session lapses into, "we already tried that and it didn't work." Here are six essentials for any ideation session.

1. *Defer judgment.* Otherwise the flow of ideas is interrupted.

2. *One person at a time.* Take turns, so that the soft-spoken but brilliant mumbler on the periphery of the room is heard.

3. *Go for quantity.* Shoot for 150 ideas in 30 to 45 minutes.

4. *Build on the ideas of others.* It's far more productive than getting 150 unconnected ideas.

5. *Encourage wild ideas.* To paraphrase Einstein, "If at first an idea doesn't sound absurd, then there's no hope for it."

6. *Go visual quickly.* Sketch ideas to help people understand them.

The payoff from ideation has become so acute that various consulting groups and individual practitioners have sprung up that specialize in helping companies spawn better ideas. One of the leading practitioners in this field is Doug Hall, a former product manager at Procter & Gamble, who runs sessions at Eureka! Ranch, in Cincinnati, Ohio. Hall promises clients 30 commercially viable ideas in three days, for which they are charged $150,000 and up for an intense three-day session. In 1997, Hall gave *Inc.'s* John Grossmann access to an ideation session designed to invent new products for Celestial Seasonings, a $75 million a year company with the lion's share of a flat market: herbal teas. Celestial wanted to double sales in the next few years, knew it must branch out beyond its present product line, and realized that every business's vitality is built on being newer and better.

Hall has, like most ideation specialists, a replicable, quantifiable process for inventing breakthrough ideas. Hall's involves a combination of play, "sensory overload," and analytical rigor. The goal is to generate as many new products and positioning ideas as possible by day's end. No idea is too radical, he tells the group. "Respect the newborns . . . tomorrow we'll strangle them." Why does he do it this way? "I do that stuff for a simple reason," says Hall. "I get better ideas. Breakthroughs are going to contradict history, so you have to break rules. It's about getting people off autopilot. You've got to shatter the systems and find new paths if you want an innovative organization," he says.

At Eureka! Ranch, overloads of stimuli in a fun environment are key to creating better ideas. Participants brainstorm in an oversized playroom, complete with video games, nerf battles, toys, and loud music from the ranch jukebox, which Hall uses to get brains pumping.

"Stimulus is the fuel that feeds business-growth thinking—or any kind of thinking, for that matter," says Hall. Stimuli include visual aids, sounds, scents, data, and experiences. Using external stimuli is more effective than using traditional "brain-draining," Hall maintains, because the stimulated brain is eager to "associate, connect, and piece together the stimuli into relevant, yet unexpected, ideas." Hall also is aided by a group of "Trained Brains" to "push for ideas that can promote an emotional reaction." These people are not formally trained; their training is the varied backgrounds and experiences they bring to the event. They "tend to be entrepreneurial types who can both dream and package their dreams into reality, and they have the ability to provoke and stimulate."

Hall's unorthodox tactics include the "Mind Dumpster," in which the first flushing of ideas are written down: new product categories, target audiences, interesting words. The point: pluck the low-hanging fruit, which is rarely the sweetest. Removing those first blush ideas frees the mind for bigger, better, more daring concepts on harder to reach branches. During brainstorming every idea is written down regardless of how outrageous it seems. From this method 1500 to 2000 ideas are typically generated. One of Hall's basic tenets is that a high number of raw ideas leads to a high number of what he calls "wicked good" ideas.

Summing up the intense three-day workshop, Hall analogizes his role to that of a football coach calling plays. "First I'll stretch their thinking from a product standpoint, focusing on occasion, target audience, etc. Then I might hit them with the picture boards, where I focus on getting them to deal with emotions and phrases and language. Now I'm getting to the marketing side. It's setting up both the running game and the passing game. We really push people here. What often happens is, late in the day, when they think they've thought of everything, all of a sudden out pops another idea."

Innovation-adept firms invest in experiencing cutting-edge ideation sessions like those held at Eureka! Ranch. They read books, attend seminars, and constantly seek to improve their skills in this area. At DuPont, for example, a special internal consulting unit contracts with the various business units on an as-needed basis to lead ideation sessions. "We've learned from the best," says Robin Karol, a manager at DuPont's Innovation Process Group. "Our process is more DuPont-like, more sedate [than some of the wackier ideation consultants the team benchmarked] but systematic. We use various methods to take people out of the box, including materials, pictures, and different methods of thinking. We use different methods depending on what country we're working in, and we are starting to do some of these sessions on the web."

Retooling Your Firm's Idea Factory for the 21st Century

There's no question that sessions led by outside ideation specialists are incredibly fun and produce a lot of new possibilities. The only downside is that, all too often, these sessions result in only momentary enthusiasm but no genuine progress. Back at the office Monday morning, other priorities and deadlines intervene. Ideas that seemed so full of potential are never acted on.

The problem is all-too-common in companies today. Ideation is not part of a disciplined, comprehensive approach to innovation. So the idea factory cannot convert raw materials into finished products, services, markets, and processes. Like a fad diet, the patient loses weight, but then quickly gains it back the minute the diet is over.

Before we move on, here are three questions to help you assess your firm's adeptness with ideation.

1. *How would you describe the way your firm's culture treats new ideas?* When the subject of innovation and creativity come up, do people air fears that "I'm not creative"? Do new ideas get analyzed immediately during meetings? If so, this tells you that there's a lot of work to be done. Outside facilitators and creativity gurus can have an impact on the culture, bringing increased awareness that, in fact, all of us are more creative than we realize.

2. *How effectively is your firm listening to customers for their ideas?* And how sophisticated is your firm presently at listening for unarticulated needs that may point you toward breakthrough ideas rather than "me too" products and service enhancements?

3. *What would it take for you personally to become your firm's ideation expert?* In other words you would become the person others come to when they realize that the ideas they have and the approaches they are taking aren't really bringing the results needed. What would you do, whom would you consult, what seminars would you attend?

It's amazing the energy and enthusiasm that result when steps are taken to activate an entire firm's culture and get the ideational juices flowing. As you ponder the suggestions in this chapter, the real question is this: Does your firm have "tons of ideas lying around" as many claim, or is the well dry? Either way, enhancing your firm's ability to generate ideas will prove beneficial, especially as it relates to producing more powerful products, which is the subject of the next chapter.

CHAPTER 7

Producing Powerful Products

People don't pay for technology. They pay for a solution
to their problem or for something they enjoy.

—Dean Kamen

Inventor of Segway Human Transporter

In a recent year, consumer-products makers churned out more than 31,000 new products in the United States alone, including multiple varieties of everything from tomato sauce to garbage bags.

Few of these products will survive. And fewer yet will succeed. The most optimistic estimate is that only one in five launches will succeed; the most pessimistic, one out of 671. Many failures result from basic miscalculations about what customers need. The product is developed for all the wrong reasons. It was the CEO's pet project. The engineers fell in love with the "really neat" technology and assumed buyers would too.

Among the more egregious examples:

- Nestea's Tea Whiz, a yellowish carbonated beverage. Hmmm, maybe a poor choice of product name?

- Ben-Gay Aspirin. Lesson: if you specialize in a product that's hot to the touch, it's probably not a good idea to attempt a line extension with a digestible version of that product.

- Premier, R.J. Reynolds Tobacco's attempt at a "smokeless cigarette" that would satisfy smokers without the health hazards. One small oversight: Smokers enjoy the smoke and the taste of burning tobacco. Premier had neither.

Driving Growth Via New Products

These firms aren't alone in introducing duds. Many firms today, both in the manufacturing and services arenas, struggle with developing new products to drive top- and bottom-line growth. The pressure to produce more new products with shorter time to market intervals and bigger payoff is enormous. Add this to the financial community's pressure for steady quarterly earnings growth and you understand how a Tea Whiz or a Ben-Gay Aspirin made it to the launch pad.

Attempts at product innovation by many companies bring to mind Samuel Johnson's description of a dog walking on its hind legs. "It is not done well; but you are surprised to find it done at all." Most firms today focus on, and have become steadily better at, taking costs out of the manufacturing operations. They focus on incremental improvements to existing products and add endless line extensions to remain at parity with competitors.

Innovation Vanguard companies set different priorities. Instead of focusing on their competition, they focus on their customers, their needs today and unarticulated needs, wants, and desires that they can satisfy tomorrow. Instead of focusing on shareholder value, they focus on creating exciting, unique *customer* value, believing that if customers are served, shareholders will be ultimately rewarded.

How Innovation-Adept Firms Approach Product Innovation

Kuczmarski & Associates is a highly respected Chicago-based new product development consulting firm. Not long ago Kuczmarski conducted a study of 209 companies' practices in new product and service management, seeking to determine the characteristics of the most successful organizations. What they found was eye-opening:

- The "best" new product companies enjoy higher rates of growth and greater profits and stock valuations than the "rest." More than three-quarters (77.8 percent) of the "best" companies believed that their new products and services processes contributed to their success. By contrast, less than a third (26.4 percent) of the "rest" said so.

- Less than half (48.8 percent) of all companies formally measure speed to market of new product/service introductions. Fewer than 5 percent of all companies (4.3 percent) measure return on innovation investment (ROII).

- A majority of companies do not formally measure new product/service success rates at all.

- The "best" new product/service firms (70.6 percent) provide more consistent and effective senior management support to new product/service development. Only 40.4 percent of the "rest" receive such support.

- The "best" are most often "market innovators" (70.6 percent) versus only 26 percent of the "rest." Forty-eight percent of the "rest" describe their new product strategy as "low risk imitation, not pioneering."

- A majority of the "best" new product/service companies (55.8 percent) are moderately or highly supportive of risk-takers during new product development. But less than one-third of the "rest" (28.1 percent) are.

- The "best" companies conduct customer-need identification research more consistently and effectively than the "rest": 37.7 percent versus 5.0 percent.

- A slight majority (52.9 percent) of the "best" new product/service companies solicits customer input and feedback prior to idea generation. But only a third (32.6 percent) of the "rest" conduct customer needs research prior to idea generation.

Six Strategies for Producing Powerful Products

Kuczmarski's study parallels the survey findings of consultancy Arthur D. Little, Inc. that we first reported in the Introduction. Recall that of 669 global executives surveyed, fewer than one in four believe their companies have "mastered the art of deriving business value from innovation."

The good news is that no matter the state of a firm's new product development processes at present, with effort that firm can revamp its approach and thereby use new products to drive growth. Here are six strategies for producing powerful, revenue-growing products:

Product Innovation 1:
Study Previous Breakthough Products

Throughout this book, we've looked at a number of breakthrough products. We've seen how some of them were the result of a *happy accident*. Nutrasweet, today a $2 billion a year product for G.D. Searle Company, was discovered by a researcher attempting to find a drug to treat ulcers. Pfizer's Viagra was "accidentally" discovered by scientists attempting to stimulate receptors in the human heart. Canon's ink-jet printer was discovered when a technician left a soldering iron on near a bottle of ink.

We've also seen how some breakthrough ideas came about because they were first to *exploit change*, as Federal Express did with its Overnight Letter product, and McDonald's did in creating a whole new range of products when it first opened for breakfast. But what to do if you want to consciously go after breakthroughs? What would you do? One answer: study previous breakthrough products.

Below is a list of breakthrough ideas, some of which we've discussed in earlier chapters and some that we haven't. What do these ideas have in common?

- 3M's Post-it Notes
- Miller Lite
- Medtronic's Pacemaker
- DuPont's Kevlar
- Pepsi's Gatorade

- Sun Microsystems' Unix Server
- Colgate-Palmolive's Total Toothpaste
- Herman Miller's Aeron Office Chair
- Gillette's Sensor Razor
- FedEx's Overnight Letter

Producing Powerful Products

1. Study previous breakthrough products.

2. Focus relentlessly on value creation throughout the development process.

3. Design and implement a new product development process.

4. Use a learning strategy for more radical ideas.

5. Use cross-functional teams.

6. Use rapid prototyping.

- Callaway's Big Bertha
- Volkswagen's Beetle
- Chrysler's PT Cruiser
- Sony's Walkman
- Merrill Lynch's Cash Management Account
- Sony's PlayStation
- Kimberly-Clark's Pull-Ups
- McDonald's Chicken McNuggets
- Palm Computing's Pilot Organizer

What do these products have in common? Let's take a look:

Breakthroughs provide a superior solution to problems the customer recognizes as problems. Gillette's Sensor razor, when launched globally in the early 1990s, became an immediate best-seller. The market—men with whiskers—was familiar to Gillette, but the new razor was so superior in producing a noticeably closer shave, that that was enough.

Breakthroughs like Sensor push the envelope in terms of effectiveness, affordability, speed, mobility, portability, convenience, customization, choice or level of service.

Breakthroughs provide a solution to problems the customer didn't recognize he or she had, until the product came along. In the 1970s and 1980s, American businesspeople began to travel more frequently as part of their jobs. In response, entrepreneurial firms invented organizer notebooks. On-the-go professionals adopted models with names like Daytimer and Filofax as a solution to a new problem: staying organized while being mobile. These products contained an address book, note-taking pages, various references, and an appointment calendar. Companies that were first movers prospered in converting the professional classes to this new solution. Then, when Palm Computing's Pilot Organizer provided these same features in a smaller, lightweight electronic device, it became a superior solution to millions of users.

Breakthroughs often resolve a contradiction. Customers often have contradictory needs. They want to drink beer but they also want to reduce caloric intake. Products like Miller Lite, along with a plethora of "low-calorie" foods, purport to help them do both. Think of any two terms that describe inexpensive or low-end products or services with those usually associated with high-end or luxury ones. By offering both, you resolve the customer's contradiction.

Kimberly-Clark listened to customers who purchased Huggies disposable diapers and stumbled upon an unresolved contradiction. Parents told researchers they didn't want their toddlers to have to wear diapers any more, even though their kids were still not toilet-trained. At the same time, they didn't want their children to have accidents or to wet the bed. Kimberly-Clark's solution, Pull-Ups, mitigated this contradiction and became an immediate breakthrough product for the firm.

Breakthroughs provide customers with an enabling new benefit often beyond the product itself. If you visit the Henry Ford Museum in Detroit, you will see, among other objects on display, hundreds of early farm machines and devices, many of which never caught on. But one of them did: Cyrus McCormick's harvesting machine, the Reaper. Was the Reaper so superior to other machines on the market at the same time? What innovation scholars believe put Cyrus McCormick's invention out ahead of the pack was a novel enabling benefit. McCormick sold to farmers on credit—a strategy innovation—allowing thousands of buyers who could not otherwise afford the machine to pay it off over time.

Henry Ford's *enabling benefit* was to continue to reduce the price of his Model T to make it affordable to the middle class. Callaway

Golf's Bertha enabled even average golfers to drive the ball farther and straighter, even if they didn't hit it with perfect form. Medtronic's Pacemaker allowed patients with heart conditions increased mobility and the opportunity to carry on with their lives, even though afflicted with a serious condition.

Breakthroughs go against conventional wisdom. Rather than succumbing to what seemed like the inevitable rise of Microsoft's Windows and Intel chips in high-powered servers, Sun Microsystems went against conventional wisdom and developed its own system instead. Sun focused its research spending on its own brand of Unix, Solaris™, and its own in-house chip, the SPARC™. When Microsoft's operating system didn't evolve fast enough and robustly enough to handle the heavy lifting required of a web server, Sun's Unix server became a breakthrough. As Unix servers became the backbone of the Web, Sun sold more of them than Hewlett-Packard, IBM, and Compaq combined.

Well, that's our list and it's only partial. What observations might you add? Identifying the qualities and characteristics of breakthrough ideas could fill the pages of a book. But you can use this partial list to stimulate your thinking about the qualities and characteristics that will describe your next product. Start by listing the recognized breakthroughs in your industry. What ideas have enlarged the pie for everybody? And more importantly, what's next?

Product Innovation 2:
Focus Relentlessly on Value Creation

Companies often maintain they want to innovate but their customers are resistant to any changes. They are risk averse, don't want new and improved, and don't want to pay higher prices for premium, value-added products. There's no question customers say this and that they believe it. What it really means is that they haven't seen strong enough reasons to pay more to satisfy their needs and go to the trouble of switching to something new. Customers naturally want to think of your products as commodities so they can negotiate the lowest price. But don't let your vision be limited by this tendency.

Instead, focus on creating a greater amount of value for the customer as you develop the new product or service. Ideas fail in the marketplace because firms lose sight of the value they deliver to customers. A relentless customer value focus needs to be at the heart and soul of every decision, every meeting, every person on the team. It's a time-honored path to success. If you analyzed a hundred break-through ideas, what you would find is that virtually every one *created new value for the customer.*

The genesis of most companies' new offerings is just the opposite. Instead of "what will this do for the customer," it's "what will this do for us?" Meaning, what will this new product do for us to raise prof-its, grow the business, make us rich, make my division look good, meet our metrics, get the CEO off my back, etc. In contrast, the mantra at innovation-adept firms is: how will it add value to our cus-tomer's life?

If your new product or service offering truly offers greater value, customers will be willing to pay for it, it's just that simple. They'll be willing to endure the "costs" associated with getting up and running with your new product. They'll be willing to take the risks to enjoy the rewards. Innovation-adept firms know that the *voice of the cus-tomer* needs to permeate the entire process, and that means that everyone on the cross-functional team, not just the idea's champion, lives and breathes customer value.

Product Innovation 3:
Design and Implement a New Product Development Process

Numerous studies have demonstrated the value of having a rigorous, embedded new product development process in place, one in which all the phases are completed and each phase is evaluated by an objec-tive committee or governance board composed of people who are not actively involved in the day-to-day project. In innovation-adept firms, new product development follows a systematic process, begin-ning with ongoing mining the future activity, and moving through various stages of development from ideation, to concept refinement, prototyping, business case analysis, development, market testing, and launch.

Typically a new product or process will have five or six check-points where the governance board issues a "go ahead" and gives fur-ther funding or kills the project outright. These checkpoints can range from as few as three to as many as ten (see Figure 5 on the next page). Maytag has only three major stages. GE incorporates ten into its process.

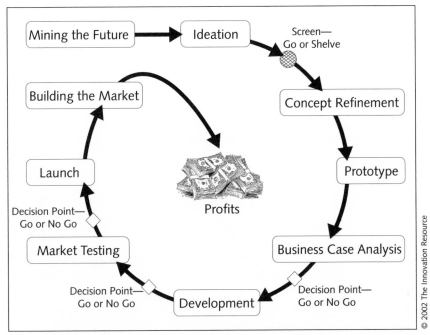

Figure 5   Representative New Product Development Process   Remember that feedback during all phases of the process is essential.

By establishing these review gates, senior management empowers development teams to do their jobs and restricts detailed financial and technical oversight to the pre-established reviews. This has the advantage of avoiding paralysis by analysis and micromanagement and decision delays, which impede progress and frustrate team members.

Robert G. Cooper, marketing professor at McMaster University, developed the "stage-gate" approach which has had a significant impact on the way many firms manage new product development. Cooper's approach often brings products to market faster, at greater success rates, and with major improvements in performance. Danger signs or weaknesses are detected earlier and cost overruns are aired. Launches are better planned. Stage Gate forces discussion of the product's definition upfront. This is important since how well the project is defined prior to entering the ensuing phases has proved to be a vital factor in later success.

Indeed, when failed products are analyzed, the invariable finding is that each functional area was busy doing its own piece of the project. But there was very little communication between players and functions, and no real commitment of players to the project, with participants having numerous other functional tasks underway at the same time. Stage-gating progress, from concept to launch, makes a cross-functional approach essential.

Before Stage Gate helped make product innovation systematic, management expectations for new product risk were often not quantified or communicated. Project teams were unaware of the company's desired risk level and new product efforts ended up never being killed.

At each Gate are descriptions of what the project/team needs to prove, know, accomplish, or better understand in order to allow the project to go forward to the next stage. Stage Gates also enable a company to halt a project before it goes too far. No-go criteria are established up front, and the project team can more easily accept rejection if criteria are not met.

Product Innovation 4:
Use a Learning Strategy for More Radical Ideas

Process-driven strategies, of which Stage Gate is the most prominent, work well for developing incrementally better products and line extensions. They work well when customers are well known and their needs and wants can be easily determined by using traditional marketing research and surveys.

Process-driven strategies work less effectively when the firm is dealing with a radical product idea or a fundamentally new business model or unproven technology. What should the criteria be at each stage? How should progress be measured, especially when there are no known customers, when the project is a drain on short-term profits, and the technology itself is unproven?

Here, a *learning-driven* strategy is called for. Most managers intuitively recognize that the development process for radical new products and services must be different from that for line extensions and incremental improvements. Yet, seldom is there a deliberate process or strategy for evaluating these projects differently. All too often, academic research shows that developers were held to standards of the normal gated project evaluation process or treated in an ad hoc fashion.

According to innovation researchers, radical projects generally evolve from projects that get repeatedly axed and restored. The product's dimensions and the market emerge gradually, as opposed to being known. Techniques such as concept testing, customer surveys, conjoint analysis, focus groups, and demographic segmentation proved in hindsight to be of limited utility and were sometimes strikingly inaccurate. Almost none had a significant impact on the development of these innovations.

"What you end up with is rarely what you started with," says Gary Lynn, associate professor at Stevens Institute of Technology. "Since the steps are not well defined, lucky discoveries and accidental findings often send the project off in new directions. Using a regular gate process doesn't work since it doesn't account for the unexpected twists and turns." Instead of the phase gate process, Lynn and others in the Innovation Movement propose an alternative process they call *probe and learn*. These scholars insist that companies can plan radical innovations, within broad guidelines, as long as they foster a spirit of team learning. By recognizing at the start that a learning strategy is called for, everyone understands the stakes much better and the nature of the pursuit. By agreeing on such a strategy, the organization can effectively develop products by probing potential markets with early versions of the products. It can also seek feedback on the probes, make adaptations, and seek more feedback, not just from customers or potential customers but from suppliers who may have valuable inputs and any others as well.

Like the phase gate processes, probe and learn is an iterative process, but one that allows for uncertainty. The firm enters a market with an early version of the product, learns as much as it can from the experience, modifies the product and marketing approach based on what it learns, and then tries again.

When GE Medical first launched a breast scanner, it failed miserably in the marketplace. But it did demonstrate the feasibility of the new technological approach: the "fan-beam" system. GE followed its breast scanner with a fan-beam–based whole-body scanner that also failed. But as before, GE's product development engineers gained valuable insights. Among them: that the marketplace was receptive to a fundamentally faster, higher resolution CT system.

Clearly, different products will require different processes. If products and technologies are truly "new to the world," if markets are new to the company, a strict, gated process may signal a "no-go" decision prematurely. It's best to custom tailor your process to fit the idea, as a one-size-fits-all approach may jettison projects with true breakthrough potential.

Product Innovation 5:
Use Cross-Functional Teams

Cross-functional teams have become the accepted standard for new product development. But what learnings tell us how best to form one?

For starters, your new product team shouldn't be chosen based on availability, but on team chemistry and fit. Pay attention also to getting the right skill-sets as well as skill-mixes into your team. Both technical and interpersonal skills are needed among team members and a mix of maverick thinkers with those who excel at execution. Finding the right people is a key priority.

Cross-functional teams bring the advantage of concurrent decision making. Concurrent engineering is not new—it was first used in Japan in the 1980s to speed product development. This powerful method involves every level of the company in basic design decisions. It enables developers to incorporate feedback from sales, marketing, accounting, manufacturing, suppliers, customers, and assembly workers early in the new product development process. There it is still cheap to fix mistakes, rather than later, once millions of dollars have been spent.

Product Innovation 6:
Use Rapid Prototyping

Product developers for centuries have used prototypes to more ably model the real thing. In recent years, with the coming of computers and sophisticated CAD (computer aided design) capabilities and the relative ease with which models can be "constructed," prototyping has become an important component in producing more powerful products.

One of the chief proponents of innovation prototyping is Michael Schrage, co-director of the MIT Media Laboratory's e-Markets Initiative, and a leading voice in the Innovation Movement. Schrage's work explores the cultures of modeling and simulation in managing innovation and risk. In one of his books, Schrage sought to discover the secrets to creative collaboration. He thought that he was looking for the "collaborative temperament" and that he would find personality traits that make collaborators effective. Instead, his key finding was that the bedrock necessity for effective collaboration is the existence of what he came to call "shared space."

"'Shared space' is the dominant medium for collaboration," Schrage says, "because it takes shared space to create shared understandings." And models, prototypes, and simulations enhance these vital shared spaces between collaborators, allowing them to "play" with ideas that make the proposed product better and better, and to go faster in exploring development possibilities at less cost. Seeing how a car crashes on a computer, Schrage argues, is much less expensive than crashing it against a wall in real life. "Likewise, it's so much cheaper to have a financial simulation that shows that the mutual fund or the synthetic security you're designing will fail in a high-interest-rate environment than to market it and have it blow up your clients' portfolios when market conditions shift because you didn't stress-test it."

To Schrage, the web is "the greatest medium for rapid modeling, prototyping, and simulation that has ever been invented." It automates and enhances information transfer, data transfer, and knowledge transfer, and Schrage argues that, most important of all, it automates the prototyping process. It's easier to play with possibilities. Suppose we change this factor?

Whatever your business, you will benefit from emphasis on prototyping early, often, and with customers.

Beta-Testing and Pilot Customers Microsoft took the use of beta-testing and pilot customers to a whole new level. Before it launched its Windows 95 software, Microsoft distributed 400,000 copies of a beta version of the software, providing it free of charge to small businesspersons, individuals, and corporate computer enthusiasts for their feedback. Eager to be in on the buzz, their participation gave them bragging rights with peers. But pilot users helped the company debug harmful errors, as well as come up with value-enhancing additional features. Microsoft was thus able to tap the creativity and gain insights of a user population that mimicked the actual market. It also shifted hard-dollar costs to these volunteers since they had to put up with bugs that had yet to be patched.

Beta-testing your new product with pilot customers can create or expand the relationship you have with a group of users and can be a win for both. Your company saves money on development costs and is able to launch a product that is more attuned to customer feedback. Customers benefit from participation as well.

How Maytag Invented Neptune, Produced a Breakthrough Product, and Reinvented Its Approach to Innovation

Change in the external environment can often spur positive responses in a firm's internal environment. Such was the case at Maytag, the Newton, Iowa appliance maker. With passage of the National Appliance Energy Conservation Act in 1987, the Department of Energy was required to set standards for maximum energy use for all major appliances. Initial standards, set in 1991, were easy to meet. But as Maytag's product developers looked ahead, they saw the real possibility of much more stringent standards being imposed on clothes washers, and they set to work to design one that would meet such standards.

The first prototype Maytag designed was simply a larger-sized European horizontal axis washer. But test consumers didn't like it compared to conventional washers. So Maytag assigned several teams to explore design options to overcome objections that people had to high-efficiency washers that were currently on the market. One of the teams developed the idea of tilting the tub up 15 degrees, opening it up much wider than prior prototypes. Market research reaction to these washers came back really strong. "This is when we started to think, 'maybe we've got something here beyond just satisfying government regulations,'" recalls Frank Nekic, Neptune's champion.

To capitalize on the unexpectedly strong reactions, Operation Lock-Up became a highly unconventional next step. For 30 days, a cross-functional group of Maytag engineers, marketing people, industrial designers, sales managers, assembly line workers, and finance people came together with all their knowledge and experience in one place. Progress was enormous. Working rapid prototypes were made that looked like real products. Additional solutions emerged; among them an integrated suspension system to minimize cabinet vibration, add stability, and offset any clothes load imbalance. In only four weeks, the team had come up with the basic ideas that would form the new product.

Next, the Neptune team fanned out to Chicago, Atlanta, and Denver with three different prototypes, seeking a hundred consumers' reactions at each site. Participants donned headsets and were shown the prototypes as an announcer provided a brief description

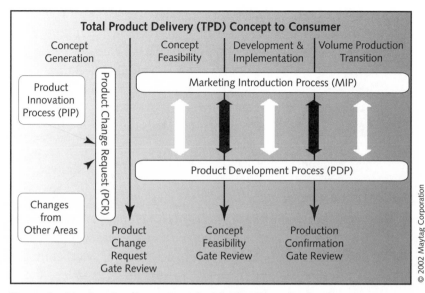

Figure 6   Maytag Appliances' product innovation process

of the product's features. Consumers were given an opportunity to load and unload clothes so they could get a feel for the ergonomics of each prototype, and then filled out a several page questionnaire on their likes and dislikes.

Later, the researchers used a promising technique called "conjoint analysis" to look at consumer reactions to variables in brand, product design, feature packages, and prices (conjoint comes from "considered" and "jointly"). As Nekic recalls:

> We would show consumers three or four designs while they sat in front of a computer: "if you have design L with the Maytag name on it with this feature package at $700, or design Z with a competing brand name on it with this feature package, which would you buy?" They'd vote for one. The computer has this algorithm that takes the ones that they prefer and presents tougher and tougher decisions for them; they go through about 16 iterations and it'll narrow it down to their two best options and make them vote at the very end on it. It will take these hundreds of consumers' tabulations and then run them through another algorithm that you have

to have a Ph.D. in statistics to work out. But it will tell you, "if there's a Whirlpool out there with this design at this price and a Maytag out there with this price, what'll be the market shares and it will spit it out for you." To give us a feel that there was some validity to it, we would compare these hypothetical findings with questions about products that were in the market already. And conjoint analysis came within one or two points of market share in the market today, so we felt there was some validity in how all this came about.

How Neptune's Developers Used Ethnography

Another approach the Maytag team gives high praise to is ethnography, which we discussed in Chapter 6. Doug Ringger, an engineer by training and Maytag's director of product planning, calls ethnography "an anthropological approach to studying consumer's use of their appliances." As he describes it:

> We would make arrangements to go into people's homes and watch them interface with their laundry appliances. So you're in the house, kids running around, they're comfortable, you try to say as little as possible and you just want to watch them do laundry.
>
> Later, you would ask open-ended questions like, "when you take your clothes out of the washer, why do you inspect them so closely?" And they might say, "Because some things I don't put in the dryer." It's a situation where were they just to verbalize, you [as a researcher] would get one picture in your mind, but when you see them actually do it, you gain deeper understanding. What you are looking for are compensatory actions, things they do to compensate for weaknesses in the product; things they just take for granted and do every day; things they'd never in the world bring them up to you as complaints or suggestions for improvement. But when you ask them, they'll say, "Oh, I do that because the washer doesn't do this or the refrigerator doesn't do that." That gives you an *unarticulated need* and that's what we're looking for.

Another compensatory behavior that was surfaced using ethnography had to do with the staggered times of completion when consumers wash and dry clothing. Some high-efficiency washers take up to two hours to wash a load of clothing. So Maytag engineers created a wash cycle time that matched closely with dryer time. "We didn't want consumers to have to come back to the laundry room at staggered times, over and over again," says Nekic.

"The real [insights] keep popping up and you say, 'wow, if we could do that for the consumer, that would be a tremendous new feature.'"

Using Pilot Customers to Gauge Response

Neptune did well in market research. But would it sell? As the launch date approached, the team wanted to know how they could get a more realistic view of what the consumer thought of the product. Maytag sells appliances through Maytag Home Appliance Centers that sell strictly Maytag products. One of their promotions throughout the year is what they call private sales, where they send a letter to their customers, announcing that on a certain evening, they'll have special pricing on Maytag, come in, bring the letter with you.

"We thought this would be a great place to show it to consumers and competitors wouldn't see it," recalls Nekic. They took prototype models to private sales in Phoenix, Spokane, and Columbus, Ohio and had them on the floor with all the others. "We'd say, 'do you mind us showing you the latest and greatest in laundry?' And we'd pitch them the product just like it was available. Maytag would give them an existing topload washer and then when Neptune became available, they would replace it with a Neptune. So we actually got people to write a check for Neptune, we got them to vote with their pocketbook and not just Monopoly money."

Such testing with pilot customers assaulted an assumption that "with the $1,000 price, they would have to gear it toward the ultra, high-income consumer and advertise it in *Metropolitan Home, Architectural Digest,* and other upscale magazines. We discovered that it had a broad based appeal," says Nekic. He added:

> People who weren't necessarily high-income consumers saw the value in this product and said, "I think it's worth it. With the savings I get per year on my utilities, I can justify to myself that this is not an extravagant item, this is something that really is a solution to problems I have in my home." There were a lot of ways we sold this product.

One was capacity. You can put in big scatter rugs, sleeping bags, comforters, that you would normally take down to the coin laundry because you don't want to do rugs in an agitator type washer. Now you can do all that stuff in your home with this washer.

Everybody had his or her own reasons for buying Neptune. One might buy it because it extracted more water, which shortened the dryer time. Now you could dry things as fast as you washed them. Some thought it looked sexy; "I just like how it looks." Others bought because it was new and different.

Neptune Spawns a New Process

What Maytag had discovered was company-changing, bedrock stuff. Innovation, driven by consumer need, will result in powerful, value-added products people will pay more for. "We made the decision that we aren't going to release any new product unless it is driven by consumer insight," says Ringger. "They had to drive it: not an engineer, not a marketing person, it wasn't somebody from sales. It was the consumer. Product innovation will be the engine that drives growth for Maytag appliances, innovation centered around consumer need."

Maytag also realized it needed a documented product development process to produce a steady stream of Neptunes in all its product categories.

"Most processes don't fail because they are poor processes," says Ringger, "but because they are not properly implemented." To strengthen the overall product development processes, a separate team was formed with representatives from each of Maytag's manufacturing sites, including cooking, dishwasher, laundry, and refrigeration. Today, all Maytag Major Appliances sites use the same process, called Total Product Delivery (TPD), in bringing new products to market (see Figure 6). A brief written description of each part of the process, flowcharts, and process templates are available to everyone. Maytag's intranet gives everyone immediate access to the process, and any changes, in real time. In-depth training sessions were held for those using the process day-to-day, with all others getting process overview training. A team is in place that works on continuous improvement of the process.

Designing Your Own 21st Century Product Strategy

If Maytag, a company once thought to be as sleepy as its "Maytag Man" spokesperson on television, can revamp its new products innovation process and drive revenue and profit growth from doing so, why not you?

Having read this chapter, now it's time to think about your company as it relates to product innovation. Jot down your responses to the following questions.

1. How would you rate the progressiveness of your firm's new product development process? What improvements have you introduced to the process, and how effectively have those changes increased top-line growth?

2. What are the breakthrough ideas in your industry that everyone recognizes? What has been your firm's strategy for discovering it's next breakthrough idea?

3. How would you characterize your industry's clockspeed and general rate of innovation? What is your customers' perception of the innovativeness of your products and services?

4. Draw a map of your current new product development process. Ask others involved to do so also. Discuss differences, points of general understanding, and ideas for improvement.

5. What role can/might you personally play in revamping the new product development process in your company?

These aren't just idle questions. In the 21st century, you can't afford to wait around for happy accidents. You can't wait for someone else to take the initiative to improve your approach to new product innovation. Nor, for that matter, can you afford to wait when it comes to generating growth strategies, and that's a subject we'll explore next.

CHAPTER 8

Generating Growth Strategies

Interesting and innovative ideas do not a business make. Getting people to pay for innovative and interesting ideas is what makes a business.

—Michael Schrage
Co-director, MIT Media Lab's e-Markets Initiative

After the fall of hundreds of dot-com firms in the early 2000s, dejected leaders were often quoted as saying, "we just couldn't seem to get our business model worked out, and we finally ran out of cash." While dot-com firms are under extreme pressure to prove the efficacy of their business models, existing firms face a challenge that is no less daunting: how to *sustain* the efficacy of their business models in the face of unrelenting change and competition.

The fact is, no matter how bulletproof your firm's current business model, it will be challenged by new business models. Over time, it will also be imitated, and thereby diluted and commoditized and copied to death.

Upstarts may or may not have staying power. Yet collectively they can render today's method of creating value for customers passé, or worse. The new reality is that business models have shelf lives, like loaves of bread at the supermarket. Companies must constantly attempt to discover new business models if they hope to survive and grow.

Hatching new business models can conjure images of well-financed whiz kids inside business incubators hovering around whiteboards, excitedly brainstorming billion-dollar breakthroughs. Yet if the dot-com crash has lessons, they may be that native genius is less than what is called for, nor can piles of venture capital ensure market acceptance.

Instead, it's useful to have deep understanding of the customers who will be expected to buy the toys, financial services, beauty products, furniture, or whatever it is that the business model purports to deliver. Indeed, case studies of successful business model innovations show that evolutionary, rather than revolutionary, ideas may have the best chances of success.

Category Killers: A Strategy Innovation Whose Time Has Come and Gone?

Fifteen years ago, the "category killer" business model was all the rage. New superstores such as Office Depot and Toys R Us collectively decimated the traditional mom and pop business model, which relied upon three-step distribution: from manufacturer to wholesaler-distributor to retailer to customer. The result was that thousands of small, independent retailers of stationery supplies, toys, hardware, sporting goods, and other products did not survive.

In recent years, the business model of the category killers themselves has been battered. At first, consumers were attracted to the huge specialty stores, with their promise of deep discounts and large selection. Over time, customers wearied of making special trips to individual specialty stores, which were often located in out-of-the-way areas. Consumers expected product knowledge from specialty store salespeople. Instead they found vast empty aisles of merchandise and clueless clerks, and left disappointed.

For the stores, maintaining a comprehensive product selection boosted inventory costs. The spread of category copycats made it impossible for stores to guarantee the lowest prices. When two or more stores in the same category competed in the same local market, there was little to differentiate them except price. Result: In one category after another, profits dwindled as competing specialty chains duked it out for survival.

"Category killers will be a diminishing force," says Richard W. Latella, senior director of the retail group at real estate marketer Cushman & Wakefield. Latella predicts that another business model, represented by Wal-Mart's supercenters, will be the fastest growing segment of retail in the coming decade. "When they build their superstores, they incorporate a lot of the categories, and they're good at execution," Latella notes.

Whether category killers will be supplanted by supercenters, or whether the supercenters themselves will be supplanted by some new business model, remains to be seen.

What is clear is that enduring business models spring from seeking to fathom the unmet and unarticulated needs that people have in a given arena of their lives, and responding with imaginative solutions.

The Evolution of Tyson Foods

When Donald Tyson took over the family poultry processing business from his father in 1971, it wasn't doing badly. With $71 million in annual sales, the business consisted of buying chicks from local farmers and raising the birds until their eleventh week. After dressing the broilers, Tyson trucked them to grocery stores in Arkansas and neighboring states.

As Tyson sought to grow the business, it became a question of how and where. Answers came cackling forth in the form of a motto that somebody tacked up on the bulletin board at the company's modest, cement-block headquarters in Springdale, Arkansas: "Do more with chicken."

"We were just processing raw chickens when we first started," Tyson told this author in a 1998 interview. "Then we started making chicken patties and that opened up a whole new area of business for us because people could have chicken sandwiches. We tapped a new market is what we did. Then, of course, we evolved into doing all sorts of things."

All sorts of things indeed. Tyson led the industry in figuring out ways to sell chicken in more forms (not just fresh, whole fryers, but also chicken pieces, marinated chicken, and frozen prepared dinners). The company then began aggressively inventing new products (chicken tenders, chicken nuggets, even a ready-to-eat chicken snack, Buffalo Wings). Actually, *invent* is not the right word; *borrow* is more accurate, as was the case with Buffalo Wings, which Tyson scouts learned about on a visit to Buffalo, New York, to learn why the company was unexpectedly selling so many chicken wings in that football-crazed city.

Tyson operatives quickly discovered that sports bars in Buffalo had created a new way to use chicken wings, because they could be purchased so cheaply. By adding flavorful sauces and serving the wings during happy hour, the taverns kept patrons around longer. Tyson adopted this idea, expanded it nationally, and created demand for a chicken part that had previously been virtually unmarketable.

Process innovations enabled the company to standardize a product that had always been inconsistent in taste and texture. Introducing factory-style farming methods, Tyson Foods was one of the first to create fresh chicken with consistent enough quality and size to carry a national brand name. The biggest breakthrough occurred when the company went all out to sell chicken into venues far beyond the grocery store channel.

Noticing that Americans were eating outside the home more and more, Tyson Foods early on realized that doing more with chicken meant making it available where people were eating—fast-food outlets, fine dining establishments, airlines, and hospitals. Tyson himself made a now-famous sales call on McDonald's Corporation in the early 1980s to persuade the company to add chicken to its menus. The result was a breakthrough for McDonald's—Chicken McNuggets—and a growth explosion for Tyson, which grew annually at rates of 36 percent for the decade that followed.

While Tyson Foods may not have consciously set out to become a strategy innovator, the company's relentless drive to "do more with chicken" transformed it into just that.

The Elements of Successful Strategy Innovation

To be considered strategy innovations, initiatives that alter a firm's business model must first turn a consistent profit. No amount of ven-

Generating Growth Strategies

1. Look for opportunities in market positioning.

2. Look for opportunities in customer outsourcing.

3. Look for opportunities in understanding customer needs.

4. Look for opportunities to reinvent your business model.

5. Look for opportunities to redefine value-added.

6. Rethink how your product or service gets into the hands of customers.

ture capital money or advertising "buzz" can substitute for that fundamental necessity. Strategy innovation has always been about solving problems for customers in ways that they, not the sponsoring company, perceive to be superior or unique from their present way of addressing those problems. Strategy innovation can be incremental, involving minor changes to the firm's business model. Or it can be a radical departure, as when a firm decides to market its existing products and services to new customer groups.

When defense contractor Hughes began its DirecTV division in the early 1990s, this was a radical departure from its existing business model, which focused on selling and servicing satellites for governments and industry. But Hughes decided to "do more with satellites" after witnessing the shrinking of defense budgets upon which it had largely depended. Hughes redeployed its expertise with satellites to pioneer a new direct-to-consumer business of beaming cable channels and movies to home satellite dishes. By 2001, DirecTV contributed 77 percent of Hughes' profits.

Strategy innovations can occur in your customer service, marketing, advertising, selling methods, or in how you distribute your offerings to end customers. Whatever their source, successful strategy innovations have one thing in common: They result from discovering new ways to create value for customers, as measured by bottom-line results to the sponsoring company. Strategy innovation may be spurred by a desire to grow ("what's in it for us"), but this desire should never be allowed to overshadow what the proposed new way of doing business will do for the customer ("what's in it for them").

Strategy innovation is, first and foremost, an act of imagination— the ability to see how something could work better from the customer's standpoint, in a way that in turn profits the sponsoring firm. New business models present themselves when companies and their leaders imagine opportunities to do more with their products and services than they have in the past.

What follows are six places to jump-start your search for imaginative new business models for your firm:

Growth Strategy 1:
Look for Opportunities in Market Positioning

What aspect of your market is not being adequately served and what might you do about it? Very simply, the imperative is: How can you hit 'em where they ain't? In many markets, commonly used phrases such as "we're high end" or "we're a discounter" point to how your firm and its product/service offerings are positioned in the marketplace, and how others who sell what you do differ on the dimensions of quality, service, and price.

Motel 6 in no way compares to Four Seasons Hotels, save that both offer guests a place to lay their heads for the night. The stripped down version of the Korean import Hyundai is not comparable to the latest model Mercedes or BMW except that both offer a means to transport human beings from one place to another via streets and roads and highways. Looking for gaps in competitor positioning involves rethinking often long-held assumptions about a company's positioning, and either adding unique or exceptional value to one's current position, or entering a different position in the following market segments:

Less for Less Southwest Airlines, from its inception, offered customers less and charged them less for it. "Less" came in the form of a scaled down level of service (no in-flight meals, no pre-assigned seating, no travel agents, no coast-to-coast nonstops). Hyundai did it with new product offerings at the very lowest end of the market.

Dollar Stores and Dollar General, both of which have prospered at the less-for-less end of the market, did so by carrying products, many of them imports, at prices even lower than Wal-Mart, K-Mart, or Target stores. Costco has pioneered ways of making this market positioning attractive to the middle class. They offer less selection breath, less convenience, less consistency of offerings, and instead sell on volume a limited, opportunistic selection and eschew service in the traditional sense.

More for More   Here, the strategic focus is on giving the customer more, meaning more service and more quality, and charging more in the process. Examples abound, from Maytag's Neptune washing machine to Tiffany to Sam Adams Beer, from Rolex watches to Dove soap to Dove Bars, from Ritz Carlton and Four Seasons to Mercedes and BMW. There's no question that this positioning strategy relies greatly on appealing to customer wants, rather than merely satisfying needs. And therein lies the biggest challenge of maintaining success while playing in this arena: You will be expected to be a leader in adding unique and exceptional value, just as you will be expected to continuously redefine "customer wants." Woe unto those that do not have the finest market-sensing antennas, who are trend followers rather than trend leaders.

Same for Less.   The extreme ends of the market aren't the whole story in positioning. Two additional positioning strategies are not only viable but are advisable, especially for new entrants in existing markets and those desiring to establish and enlarge market reach. Same for less is just such a positioning strategy. While this is the traditional appeal of the "sale," it is the fundamental strategy of Men's Wearhouse, the Fremont, California, men's clothing retailer. While many men's suit retailers have shuttered their doors in recent years due to declining sales of business suits and the trend toward more casual dress, Men's Wearhouse has aggressively expanded and has, in some cases, taken advantage of huge drops in the cost of retail space. Men's Wearhouse also provides more for less by including free pressing and follow-up calls to determine the level of satisfaction. Highly visible television advertising raises the company's profile.

More for Same   When Virgin Atlantic started up in the early 1990s, the airline knew it had to offer a noticeably superior value proposition to get travelers to switch from then-dominant British Airways. Why would passengers, especially business travelers accumulating frequent flyer miles on BA, want to try a different brand? Virgin introduced the attention-getting Upper Class service, which offered the larger seats and leg room of traditional first class at the price of business class service. Virgin further enhanced its value proposition by offering to pick up and deliver Upper Class passengers from and to their destinations. And it continues to freshen its value-added extras, most recently with onboard masseuses.

Growth Strategy 2:
Look for Opportunities in Customer Outsourcing

The operative strategy here is look for opportunities in meeting customers' ever-expanding desires to outsource their chores, tasks, and responsibilities to focus their time in more productive and meaningful ways elsewhere. This driving force of change shows up in both business-to-consumer and business-to-business relationships. The advance of the service economy in general, and service businesses in particular, is the story of companies and entrepreneurs imagining ways of creating customer value via outsourcing tasks consumers formerly had to do themselves.

Take the chore of changing the oil in your car. In 1980, American car owners either changed their own or brought their cars to dealers or local mechanics, an often time-consuming chore. Ten years later, 70 percent of car owners outsourced this ritual to a newly created service business, the quick lube industry.

The industry was invented in the late 1970s by a former Baltimore football coach who grew frustrated with the inconvenience of existing solutions. Jim Hindman designed Jiffy Lube to give motorists a way to solve their problem that was quick—a 10-minute time guarantee—and inexpensive. Result: Jiffy Lube grew quickly into a national chain.

Having discussed how consumers gladly outsource their chores and responsibilities when the value is perceived to be attractive, contradicting this trend has potential also. Value innovator Home Depot avoided the category killer duke-out by focusing on the unmet and unarticulated needs of homeowners. Home Depot easily undercut local hardware stores on price, while offering greater selection and knowledgeable associates who, in some cases, have real-world experience in carpentry, tile-setting, etc.

Home Depot did not achieve its phenomenal growth merely by taking market share from mom and pop hardware stores, however. It created a larger market for its wares by tapping pent up demand. People wanted to make repairs on their homes, but often lacked either the skills to do it themselves or the funds to outsource such projects to contractors. Home Depot's strategy innovation was to empower customers through knowledge-exchange: giving them the know-how and confidence that they could regrout the kitchen tile, or paint the living room, or install that drip irrigation system in the yard.

Growth Strategy 3:
Look for Opportunities in Understanding Customer Needs

All too often, competition in an industry tends to coalesce around accepted notions of market positioning from high end to unbundled low end. But these commonly accepted assumptions often extend to the basis of appeal of a product category, as either providing entertainment and/or emotional-support value, or problem-solving value. Such definitional rigidity does two things: It keeps us from imagining alternative possibilities for our offerings, and it keeps us from anticipating the emerging needs and unarticulated desires of consumers, which lie dormant, waiting to be addressed.

In developed countries, most basic consumer needs are largely satisfied. A hierarchy of *wants* supplants psychologist Abraham Maslow's hierarchy of *needs*. The quest for survival gives way to a quest to improve your standard of living, which morphs into a quest for a higher quality of life. In probing for consumer wants rather than needs, new possibilities present themselves all the time.

Say, for example, that you run a mid-sized dental practice and you are faced with declining revenues because of fewer patient visits. Americans have fewer cavities these days than ever before, which is good news for them, bad news for you. Do you look for ways to attract more customers? Or do you try to "do more with dentistry"?

One new strategy might be to get into teeth-whitening. Already a $600 million industry, it is growing at 20 percent a year, according to the American Academy of Cosmetic Dentistry. BrightSmile is a fast-growing chain of stand-alone teeth-whitening centers. "There's a whole movement taking place from fix-me dentistry to transform-me dentistry, from fill-my cavity to change-my-smile," says a spokesperson for the American Society for Dental Aesthetics in New York City, an international organization for cosmetic dentists.

Growth Strategy 4:
Look for Opportunities to Reinvent Your Business Model

Frustrated with the high prices, bureaucracy, and poor customer service of the auto insurance industry, California's voters passed Proposition 103, mandating auto insurance premium rollbacks and introducing other reforms. As we saw in Chapter 5, the 1988 measure forced insurers to rebate millions of dollars to customers and forced drastic survival measures on an embittered industry.

One company, Progressive Insurance, turned this voter-tossed lemon into lemonade and reinvented their very business model. "It was a wake-up call," says Peter Lewis, Progressive's chairman. "I decided that from then on, anything we did had to be good for the consumer—or we weren't going to do it."

Progressive responded by reinventing auto insurance from the ground up. Before, Progressive claimants waited weeks while their paperwork languished in some adjuster's in-box. These days, Progressive settles the claim with its client on the spot, no matter when the accident happens, 24 hours a day, seven days a week. The company often settles claims before other companies even know there's been an accident. Progressive's 1-800-AUTO PRO service quotes the firm's rates to potential customers—along with the rates of competitors, even if competitors' rates are cheaper.

And Progressive continues to think unconventionally in seeking to make its business model more alluring. In one pilot program, Progressive customers pay for insurance based on when, where, and how much they drive. Normally, prices are based on risk posed by a driver's age, record, marital status, and other criteria. But Progressive maintains those factors are less important than things like how much a car is used and where it is driven. "A mile driven at eight in the morning is safer than a mile driven at midnight," says a company spokesperson.

So now Progressive has been monitoring the miles—and routes—of participating Texas drivers via a tracking box affixed to their cars. The device uses cellular phone and satellite technology to monitor miles and times the car is driven each day. Billing works much like a home's gas meter. The company says premiums for Houston drivers have dropped an average of 25 percent.

Whether this experiment becomes Progressive's business model remains to be seen. But it is exactly this willingness to question long-held industry assumptions that has put Progressive in the driver's seat. Progressive has been growing at an average rate of 16 percent annually, compared to the industry's average of 3.6 percent, and it has achieved profit margins of 8 percent, whereas the industry as a whole has run at an underwriting loss over the past five years.

Growth Strategy 5:
Look for Opportunities to Redefine Value-Added

Before J.D. Power and Associates came along, the research industry defined the market for information research, and "the way we do business in this industry" in one way. Market research companies would call upon customers to obtain research contracts, which they would then conduct on a proprietary basis.

Power turned the equation upside down. Bearing all the costs up-front himself, he investigated their customers' experience and then sold his findings to the car companies for a hefty price. Customer satisfaction standouts were given the right—for an added fee—to advertise the results. Only if they paid for the research did they have the right to claim that they were "number one in customer satisfaction." A typical J.D. Power study includes 40 makes of cars, but Power publishes only the rankings of the brands that score above average. Those that finish below average are listed alphabetically in the results that are released to the public.

Growth Strategy 6:
Rethink How Your Product or Service Gets to Customers

L'eggs pantyhose built a market for itself by distributing its product in nontraditional outlets such as supermarkets and convenience stores. Amway, Mary Kay, Tupperware, and Avon all, in their own way, innovated new business models in distribution. And the dozens if not hundreds of new multilevel marketing companies that are started each year ride this wave.

Dell Computer did not follow the traditional two-step distribution, but pioneered a new business model. Dell chose not to distribute its products through the then-standard channel—to wholesalers or resellers, who sold to retailers, who then sold to end-customers—but instead sold directly to end-customers. Other innovations rounding out Dell's unique business model were strategic in nature as well: From the beginning, Dell didn't manufacturer a single computer until it received a customer's order. Because it manufactured products to order, Dell didn't have to create an inventory of standardized products to be stored until sold in one warehouse or another.

Similarly, eBay represents strategy innovation when compared to the way in which people searched for odd items such as used John Deere tractor seats and early 20th century toothbrushes.

Jump-starting Strategy Innovation at Your Firm

While these and many other strategy innovations relied on technology to change the game, not all strategy innovation is based on technology, nor does it need to be. Viable business models require imagination and passion in seeking to solve customers' problems in superior ways, rather than simply pumping up our own balance sheets. While it is all too easy to dream about creating value for ourselves, successful strategy innovators with names like Ford and Walton and Tyson seem to think deeply about creating superior value for customers.

To jump-start strategy innovation in your firm, first you must foster a willingness to rethink your understanding of how your customer receives value from you. Your business model is simply a description of how your company creates value for customers that in turn generates revenue and profits for your company. Use the six ideas from this chapter to jump-start your search for new ways to strengthen your firm's business model. Be prepared for growth, increased profitability, and sustained competitive advantage to be the result.

CHAPTER 9

Selling New Ideas

I never want to invent anything I can't sell.
—Thomas Edison

Sure, innovation is critical, but it doesn't amount to anything
unless the rest of the world does something with it.
—Douglas Engelbart
Inventor of the computer mouse

Innovation has always been about selling new ideas. An innovation, by its nature, is something different. It requires getting used to. Somebody has to help it "catch on." Innovators throughout history have willingly and ably embraced the need to sell their ideas to a skeptical world.

Thomas Edison didn't just develop direct current electricity. He trained a team of salespeople to go door-to-door demonstrating the advantages of lighting your home with electric lights. To lessen the consumer's perceived risk, Edison promised prospective customers that if they weren't completely satisfied, he would remove the wiring and reinstall kerosene lamps at no charge.

Walter Chrysler was frozen out by General Motors and Ford from exhibiting his maiden car, the Chrysler Six, at the industry's annual exhibition. Undaunted, he quickly rented the lobby of the New York hotel where most attendees would be staying and exhibited his automobile there, creating even more attention for his launch.

Selling Strategies for the 21st Century

Innovation in the 21st century requires that you and your firm master a sophisticated, multifaceted set of selling skills that are needed both internally and externally to build the buy-in and get the idea happening in the world.

Internally, this means the idea's sponsors, led by a champion, who in turn leads a cross-functional team, are successful in getting it funded, approved, and accepted. They gain buy-in from all internal players in the organization and from suppliers, alliance partners, distributors, and channel partners. All have the power to assist or kill the idea, depending on their support. Most importantly, gaining internal buy-in means gaining continuing support from senior managers (or fellow senior managers, if you are part of senior management) in the organization to support and fund the idea and otherwise help it along.

Externally, building the buy-in means gaining acceptance for the idea in the marketplace such that it sells. Decision makers decide on it. Purchasing directors purchase. Customers buy it. It produces top- and bottom-line revenue growth.

Are you ready to perform this final act necessary for successful innovation? This chapter will help you build upon the competencies you and your firm already have in this area. But be forewarned: Far from being a mere afterthought or something that, once the idea is ready for launch, can be thrown over the wall to the sales team, selling an innovation is critical to the idea's success. Developing the skills of selling ideas, both internally and externally, must be viewed as a vital part of a firm's embedded, systematic innovation process. It must become everyone's responsibility. It must become part of the discipline of innovation. And it must be seen as a vital part of a comprehensive approach to driving growth through innovation.

The Bottleneck Clogging the Pipeline, or Why Selling Ideas Is a Growing Challenge

Fast-forward to the future for just a moment and imagine your company having integrated and embedded an innovation strategy into its operating processes. Congratulations! You did it! Your company has become super-adept at organization and you can launch major innovations every couple of months.

The next question becomes: *Could your customers possibly handle that rate of innovation coming at them?* The probable answer: no. The innovation pipeline doesn't do you any good if it bottlenecks at the customer end. If new products and services emerge faster than customers can absorb, you don't get top-line growth; you get failure.

Any innovation process must necessarily concern itself with the issue of customer acceptance. How long does it take all your various customers, channel partners, gatekeepers, and end-users to integrate your new products and services? To amortize the costs? To find the time to learn how to use your new ideas? And what can you do at the beginning of the pipeline to accelerate the customer's ability to derive value from your ideas at the end of the pipeline?

The growing reality is that there are simply too many ideas—albeit, incremental improvements and line extensions—chasing consumers with finite resources, and a finite ability or motivation to adopt them all.

Here's why:

- *The customer's basic needs have been met.* In developed countries, at least, basic problems have been solved by existing products, or so the consumer thinks. Thus, future innovations from your company will arise from seeking out unarticulated customer needs. Moreover they will increasingly demand that you build the market for new ideas because, for customers to derive benefits, behavior change on their part is required.

- *Customers face overchoice.* The Consumer Electronics Association estimates that more devices will have been launched from 1998 to 2003 than during the entire previous history of the industry. Kellogg's Eggo waffles come in 16 flavors. Procter & Gamble markets 72 varieties of Pantene hair care treatments. Kimberly-Clark's

Kleenex tissue comes in nine varieties. S.C. Johnson's Ziploc garbage bags offer twist, drawstring, or handle ties. The result of such proliferation is to produce a bewildering condition commonly called *overchoice*, a term coined by futurist Alvin Toffler in his 1970 book, *Future Shock*.

- *Customers have upgrade fatigue.* Computer manufacturers and software makers are "struggling to deliver meaningful-enough innovations to keep users regularly upgrading their PCs and programs," reports the *Wall Street Journal*. "My people tell me there has not been a compelling reason to go to [Microsoft's new version] for our business requirements," one corporate purchasing official was quoted as saying. It isn't just the computer or software industries that are affected.

- *Customers resist the costs of planned obsolescence.* Early adopters in the software and hardware arenas have lured customers all too often into a cynical cycle of planned obsolescence by developers. Customers see that other industries are attempting to do the same thing, and they are attempting to stem the trend before it blossoms. Purchasing the DVD player means that your library of VHS movies is suddenly rendered obsolete, as well as your VCR. As more and more offerings are brought forth that make ever more fatuous claims, the vast middle of adopters becomes more and more skeptical by the day.

Seven Strategies for Selling New Ideas

Count on new ideas facing greater customer scrutiny and resistance, the newer and more unfamiliar they are. The days when you could build a better mousetrap and customers would beat a path to your door are over.

Given these changing realities, emphasis must be given to the skills and techniques of selling new ideas. Let's look at seven strategies for doing exactly that:

Selling Strategy 1:
Make Everyone an Idea Evangelist

Guy Kawasaki's business card at Apple Computer said simply, "evangelist." It was Kawasaki's job to talk up Apple's new products to the

Selling New Ideas

1. Make everyone an idea evangelist.

2. Focus on the customer's mean time to payback.

3. Make it safe for customers to experiment.

4. Sell conceptually.

5. Build markets for your products and services.

6. Convert the early adopters and gatekeepers first.

7. Be persistent.

media, and to appear at trade shows such as Comdex and Apple's own annual gathering of users and developers to create good feelings.

Anybody who ever hopes to be effective as an innovator would do well to emulate Kawasaki's style. The word *evangelist* might conjure an image of drawling preachers bringing sinners to repentance, but it is their devotion to their mission that perhaps caused those in the Innovation Movement to adopt the term, for they too must gain converts. In our interviews with initiative leaders in the Innovation Vanguard firms studied for this book, these leaders clearly recognize the need to "build the buy-in" lest the initiative fail. Innovation-adept firms not only take selling seriously, they "unleash the inner evangelist" in everyone, realizing that everything has to be sold.

- *Evangelists master the art of persuasion.* They know how to use the right message with the right audience at the right time. They work on communication skills and on energizing their briefings, descriptions, board reports. They join organizations like Toastmasters to improve their speaking skills. Evangelists know how to craft their messages so that people pay attention.

- *Evangelists focus on benefits, not features.* Benefits are what every salesperson learns to focus on, addressing the issue of "what's in it for me?" Not how the idea will work, not its features, but what it will do for those it is supposed to bring added value to. Will it create additional customer satisfaction because it brings about greater speed or convenience? Will it reduce costs without reducing customer delight? Will the idea raise employee morale or make the workplace a little more fun? Will it increase safety, aid efficiency?

- *Evangelists use skeptical thinkers to get the bugs out of their pitch.* While positive thinkers and possibility thinkers are prone to like your idea no matter how far-fetched, they can actually lead you astray. They'll tell you that it's a great idea regardless of the flaws. But when you seek out skeptical thinkers, you're bound to get another perspective on your idea.

- *Evangelists help others visualize new ideas.* Once you've done your homework and have isolated the benefits, you're ready to get feedback on your idea. Start with friends, teammates, mentors, and other people whom you trust to be forthright but sympathetic.

  The key thing you want to do is help them to see your vision for what could be. You want to draw a picture, create PowerPoint slides, anything that is visual and provides a common reference point other than just the talking head. The more others can feel, taste, touch, and see the idea represented, as if it's already a reality, already operational, the greater your selling success. Effective communication is half the battle. People don't like to admit that they "don't get it," that they don't understand your idea, that it's too complicated. But as every evangelist knows, if people don't understand, they don't buy.

- *Evangelists speak the language of the people they are selling to.* How you "sell" an idea depends to a great extent to whom you're selling it. If you're making a pitch to senior management about an idea management funding committee, that's a different sales job than presenting an idea to your team. It's a different sales job if you've been invited to present an idea to the board of directors. Effective evangelists find out as much as they can about the thinking styles of those they are pitching. If you have a mix of people, such as marketing, sales, human resources, finance, information technology, and other specializations, you'll need to incorporate various devices to satisfy each member of the group.

Think about the personality style of the person or persons you'll be presenting your idea to. Are they analytical? Do they tend to be more comfortable with changing the system or perfecting it? Analytical persons need the data and numbers that make the case for your idea. If your audience is more "big picture" oriented, don't bog them down with too many arcane details. They realize all these things have to be worked out. Instead, make sure you demonstrate how the idea is in alignment with the firm's growth targets, how it utilizes the firm's core competencies. Use their hot button words. No matter who the audience is, be crystal clear in the way you describe your ideas so that nobody gets left behind in all the complexity. Remember: People must buy you before they'll ever buy your idea.

Selling Strategy 2:
Focus on the Customer's Mean Time to Payback

As companies focus on driving growth through innovation, they often concern themselves with mean time to payback—how long before we see a return on our investment in this new product, service, or market. Innovation-adept firms focus instead on their *customer's mean time to payback*. What this means is how long will it take their customer to begin enjoying the benefits of their investment in your new product or service.

Not all products or services have a high mean time to payback implicit with their adoption. Purchasing Gillette's Mach3 razor and learning how to use it takes the consumer only a few minutes. Trying a new type of cold cereal, ditto. Purchasing a PT Cruiser from Chrysler, same thing.

But consider the following products and the changes required by the customer to enjoy the benefits promised:

- Whirlpool's Personal Valet is a cabinet-sized clothes refresher that removes odors and wrinkles using a chemical formula developed by Procter & Gamble. To be successful, Whirlpool must sell consumers an appliance they have never heard about, and they must learn a new approach to garment care. The valet will not remove stains, but it will take out wrinkles and deodorize clothes in 15–30 minutes.

- Athough *USA Today* enjoyed phenomenal circulation growth and popularity among readers during its initial years of operation, advertisers were slow to accept the paper, since it was the first general interest daily newspaper that was sold nationally.

- Ralston Purina's SecondNature is a new-to-the-world product: a housetraining system for pet owners of dogs under 20 pounds.

- AutoNation's attempt to provide consumers with used car superstores. The only problem, in quickly rolling out the concept without adequate testing, was that executives failed to see that used car shoppers liked purchasing locally and didn't want to drive far from home to shop.

Indeed, miscalculations at Webvan brought about its demise.

Webvan's Faulty Assumptions   In its brief, unhappy existence, the one thing that online grocer Webvan did not lack was boldness. The Foster City, California grocery delivery company quickly opened operations in 10 metropolitan areas in the United States, raised $800 million in capital, built a huge $40 million warehouse in Oakland, California, and signed a billion dollar contract to build 25 more across the country.

The size of seven football fields, the Oakland facility immediately became the world's most advanced food factory, moving the equivalent stock of 17 supermarkets along miles of conveyor highways studded with scanners to track and direct every wine bottle and box of cereal. Nine massive carousels each moved 5000 bins of products into place automatically for easy stocking.

Like many a failed idea, Webvan's underlying assumptions—"build it and they will come"—turned out to be false. Yes, there were customers who valued the convenience of not having to go to the grocery store. But they did not sign up in nearly the numbers that Webvan needed to justify investments.

In retrospect, one of the key things that Webvan's designers apparently failed to understand was consumer behavior. For many shoppers, delegating the intimate task of foraging for food wasn't something large numbers of them were willing to do at the drop of a hat. Squeezing fruit and eyeing just the right cut of pork loin involved making choices that they apparently didn't believe could be turned over to others. "This isn't like book purchasing," one of many analysts was quoted as saying. "To get people to change their behavior on something this important to their lives is very difficult."

Webvan isn't alone in needing to study the amount of change an idea will require to be accepted and used by customers. Most innovations require customers to make a change, and ascertaining their willingness to do so should be determined early in the idea's development. Training your dog to use Ralston Purina's SecondNature litter box takes time. Integrating General Electric's new speed cooker, Advantium, into your kitchen usually requires the added expense and hassle of hiring an electrician to install 220 volts. Integrating shortened cooking times for items ranging from baked potatoes to roasts requires adaptations in your cooking style. Converting to grocery shopping via an online grocer is supposed to free up your time, but takes time learning the new way.

Inertia is a huge force, as the time and trouble to switch vendors, banks, or insurance provider means that customers will overlook or forgive all sorts of customer service slights, and despite the billions spent on advertising to convince customers that they will be better off once they have begun to use your product or service. Add to this prevailing attitude the customer's creeping cynicism about what the payoff will actually be in terms of enhancing their quality of life. How much better off will your life be once you have internet access in your car? While people often become early adopters for status reasons, how much do they really need to enhance their self-esteem in this manner?

Selling Strategy 3:
Make It Safe for Customers to Experiment

An innovation, as we've said, offers a different value proposition to the buyer that says, "the way you're solving your problem today is not as good as the way you could be solving that problem." But it also suggests to customers that they trade the security and safety of the way they solve their problem today with a new way that has potential dangers. It suggests, in other words, that they take a risk, a leap from the known to the unknown. That's why it's essential to put yourself in your customers' shoes and ease their discomfort with risk-taking

Some suggestions:

- *Promise safe experimentation.* How can you make reversibility a way to get people to experiment with your idea? The age-old "money back guarantee" is certainly one way, but what about others?

- *Use familiar terms.* Early automakers used the term *horseless carriage* to get people to convert to the automobile. Thomas Edison, when he was attempting to convert people to using his electric lights, used familiar terms, and called them lamps.

- *Encourage free trial.* Starbucks often gives out samples of new beverages. Art Fry and his team at 3M gave out Post-it Notes to administrative assistants to encourage people to try the newfangled product. Give people reassurance that they can easily go back to the old way of doing things if they don't like your new way. This lowers their resistance, and hopefully the results they achieve with your new way more than make up for the costs of shifting to your new way of doing things so they don't wish to go back.

- *Make purchase easier.* As we saw in Chapter 7, Breakthrough Products often come with an enabling benefit that makes it affordable. Cyrus McCormick sold his harvesting machine to farmers on credit—a strategy innovation that allowed thousands of farmers to pay him off over time.

Selling Strategy 4:
Sell Conceptually

No matter how obvious the benefits, few ideas gain easy acceptance. You'll experience resistance, and sometimes you may not be able to tell exactly where it's coming from, both internally and externally. You'll encounter problems that you never could have foreseen. The market will react totally differently from what you or anyone on your team expected. So the experienced innovator knows to expect the unexpected and expect to have to continue to overcome objections, sell skeptics, and deal with the unexpected.

In the early 1970s, GE Medical began a project to develop Computerized Axial Tomography, CAT scan technology for short. To get feedback from lead customers, the company invited eleven of the country's leading radiologists to the Bahamas for a seven-day focus group. GE's product developers wanted these potential adopters to help them determine possible applications for their product. These radiologists turned out to be extremely skeptical. "A small, niche opportunity," was their uniform conclusion.

To its credit, the GE team pressed on, and in 1975, with its development effort well underway, they again sought the input of radiologists, this time in an attempt to determine how many hospitals were likely to buy CT systems. Tom Lambert, responsible for marketing the new product, recalls the radiologists' reaction:

"I'd say, 'This [CT] machine will to do this and this.' Their first question would be, 'How much resolution does it have?' And when I told them it had one-tenth of what they were using at the time, that was the end of the story. It took me several months to figure out what the problem was. Their view was, 'I've been taught this way in medical school and this is how you do it. It's always been done that way, always will be done that way. It works fine.' They recognized their problems as being adequately addressed by available technology, so they didn't see a need for a new technology and wondered why I was wasting their time."

As it turned out, that wasn't the end of it. General Electric's CT machines became a highly successful breakthrough product for GE Medical—but not until the team learned to sell conceptually.

Marketing an innovation, both internally and externally, depends on convincing people to adopt a new idea, but more importantly it demands that they change. Adoption of your idea is a learning process. It is undertaken either because it is required of the individual—by one's manager, say, or voluntarily, based on a complex set of beliefs, feelings, motives, and motivations, from "desire to impress others" to "not wanting to appear behind the times."

But such resistance is to be expected with truly new ways of doing things, no matter what the promised benefits, no matter the strength of the proffered value proposition.

Selling Strategy 5:
Build Markets

Developing new markets can sometimes be a slow, tedious process, yet when you do build a market, you are more apt to own that market. The impediments to building new markets are well established: Customers are not anxious to substitute a new, unknown solution for one that is tried and true. They perceive the risks, correctly or incorrectly, as being too great.

Sometimes companies must learn this lesson the hard way, as was the case at DuPont. Working at DuPont's experimental station in Wilmington, Delaware, chemist Stephanie Kwolek developed a mixture of liquid crystal polymers that performed like nothing she and her colleagues had ever seen. "We had it tested for strength and stiffness, and when the properties came back, we were amazed they were so high," Kwolek told one interviewer. The new fiber had a tensile strength modulus of 450. Nylon, by contrast, has 55. It was five times stronger than steel.

Kwolek's 1971 patent, co-held with Paul Morgan, was for a fiber DuPont named Kevlar. It revolutionized the synthetics industry and made billions of dollars for DuPont. Today Kevlar is everywhere—in police vests, army helmets, tennis rackets, mooring lines for cruise ships, skis, trawling nets, golf clubs, and racing sails. Kevlar gloves protect the hands of fishermen, auto workers, motorcyclists, gardeners, and oyster shuckers. Loggers wear Kevlar chainsaw chaps, and heads of state often wear Kevlar vests and raincoats. Embassies decorate with Kevlar curtains that can shield occupants. But breakthrough status was long in coming because, former insiders say, DuPont was stuck in the "build it and they will come" paradigm. When DuPont invented nylon, Dacron, Teflon, and many other fibers, that's exactly what had always happened. Nylon stockings went on the market in 1940, and women stood in line overnight outside their local hosiery shops so they could be the first to own a pair. Nylon made silk stockings all but obsolete and demand soared for the new material. But Kevlar customers didn't come.

One of the initial new applications for Kevlar was supposed to be the tire industry. The future looked bright, so bright that Kevlar's champions convinced senior management to build the first commercial plant, capable of making 45 million pounds of the fiber a year. But soon after construction started, tire manufacturers chose steel. Kevlar was too expensive, they concluded, and besides, car owners were attracted to the phrase "steel-belted radials."

After tire makers turned Kevlar down, DuPont was dumbstruck. "Kevlar was the answer," recalls a marketing manager for the fiber, "but we didn't know for what." Having never had to go out and build the market for its innovations, DuPont floundered. The disjointed search to find uses for the new product took over a decade and $900 million in capital to pull off.

The search for uses involved numerous missteps and missed opportunities. Instead of DuPont seeing a possible use for its fiber being protective vests for police officers, it was the other way around. A crusader for lifesaving devices from the National Institute of Justice made that connection. The vests became so popular that some policemen, and even their wives, bought them with their own money when the departments didn't have the funds. And instead of DuPont seeing a possible use for Kevlar in the military, it was the U.S. Army, shopping for a fiber to replace nylon in flak jackets, who came calling.

Belatedly, DuPont's management saw the need to reinvent its market-building process. Market niches in protective vests and racing tires were fine, but tons of new applications were needed to justify the huge investment and to build Kevlar into a breakthrough that would drive significant top-line growth. Before, market-building efforts had been piecemeal at best. But Kevlar was a turning point. DuPont realized the value of building markets, rather than waiting for markets to develop. The Kevlar group organized classes to teach itself how to sell ideas and then fanned out to call on potential users.

DuPont learned that the more innovative the product or service, the more likely it is that you must build a market for your offering. And to do that, the more essential it is to have a plan for building the market, even though your plan will have to be altered time and again. What markets will you penetrate first? How will you convert customers? How much time will it take?

Building markets for your products and services is the essence of innovation. Sometimes in the midst of obstacles you will wonder why you are going to all the trouble. Then, it is important to keep in mind the old adage: no pain, no gain. Remember: When you build a market, so long as you keep on innovating and don't rest on your laurels, you are more likely to own the lion's share of that market.

Selling Strategy 6:
Convert the Early Adopters and Gatekeepers First

Consider how the market developed for pocket calculators in the 1970s. Scientists and engineers were the early adopters of this product—it had clear advantages over the slide rule and log table—and they could easily justify the hefty price tags on early calculators. But even in these specialized markets, acceptance of calculators didn't happen overnight. No doubt some engineers determined to ignore these new devices.

Buyers learn about new products and services from a wide variety of sources, of which advertising is said to be one of the least credible. Most credible? Personal testimonials from respected friends, colleagues, and coworkers who speak from personal experience. Indeed, peer pressure to "try it, you'll like it," is often at the top of lists of why people, following on the heels of the early adopters, decide to change. The desire not to appear "behind the times" is one reason consumers vote for the new way. Who are the gatekeepers that control and influence acceptance of your idea? Convert them first.

Selling Strategy 7:
Be Persistent

The 3M team responsible for launching Post-it Notes was growing desperate. Senior management was threatening to kill the product as a loser. The product was out there in a few stores, but nobody was buying it. Getting retailers to stock the product was proving to be nearly impossible. Retailers didn't understand the product, their customers weren't clamoring for them, and who needed these silly little stacks of paper when you could just use scratch paper? What to do?

"Boise," someone suggested. And so the team responsible for the fledgling product took suitcases of the little sticky pads to the business district of Boise, Idaho, handing them out to passersby. It was a turning point; people started sticking them everywhere, finding uses, and they began asking for them at retail stores. The rest, as they say, is innovation history. Post-it Notes have brought additional billions to 3M's top and bottom line and became a sort of icon of this final ingredient of the innovation process.

How Colgate's Total Dethroned Crest and Became America's Top Toothpaste

In its first month of being launched in the North American market, Colgate-Palmolive's Total toothpaste unseated long-reigning Crest to become the best-selling product in its category. Industry observers were universal in their praise of the product, which was called the biggest advance in oral care since fluoride was added to toothpaste in the 1950s. But they were even more lavish in praising Total's launch, calling it one of the most spectacularly successful selling jobs in consumer product history. What Total did—the steps it took—provides us with important insights into selling new products and services in the 21st century and driving top- and bottom-line growth accordingly.

Behind every Breakthrough Idea, there is a team of people whose passion, commitment, and selling savvy is unsurpassed. Two hundred person Team Total had one additional advantage: the leadership of veteran product manager Jack Haber. *BrandWeek* once described Haber as a "discreetly ponytailed mensch, who seems to transcend the stereotype of a typical buttoned-up, high-powered executive, whose charm makes the impossible seem doable, even effortless, even a task as monumental as taking a blast at the reigning king of oral care."

Unseating Crest was hardly a slam-dunk. The product's development had been expensive and suffered a lengthy delay as the federal Food and Drug Administration weighed approval. Haber and his team had asked for and received $120 million for the introduction alone, making it the most expensive product launch in Colgate's history.

Over the previous decade, the U.S. oral care market had been deluged with line extensions and incremental improvements. Consumers were jaded by endless claims for pastes that whitened, eradicated tartar, controlled bad breath, and aided in gum care. But through it all, Crest was barely bruised, steadily holding the number one position since it pioneered fluoride 35 years before, just as baby boomers were getting their first molars. That turned out to be Crest's vulnerable spot. Crest's brand managers had apparently begun to believe their product, having withstood attacks from a slew of competitors, would always remain number one.

What would it take to get those boomer consumers to look past the "look ma, no cavities" history with Crest and switch brands? Total's bold answer: new benefits and a product that truly added new value.

Like Crest's fluoride, Total contained a revolutionary new ingredient, Triclosan, a highly soluble antibiotic that with two daily brushings provided round-the-clock protection against gingivitis, plaque, cavities, tartar, and bad breath. Total's developers had discovered a way to bind Triclosan to teeth. (Patents for this unique bonding process guarantee Colgate exclusivity until 2008.)

After extensive reviews of Colgate's clinical data, the FDA allowed Total to make first-ever claims for protection against gingivitis and plaque. These new benefits gave the product's marketers unique bragging rights, but would consumers listen? With all the competitors' line extensions and gimmickry in the category, launching the product would need a unique approach to convince consumers that this one was not just another pseudoinnovation, but was truly new and truly improved.

Building Buy-in Among Gatekeepers First

Upon winning FDA approval, the key question then became how to rise above the chatter of competing claims and communicate Total's unique benefits to harried U.S. consumers? Colgate-Palmolive's research indicated that two out of three consumers believed that a "fresh, clean mouth" was one of the top reasons for buying a particular toothpaste brand. But that hardly unearthed an unarticulated need that Total could latch onto.

To gain their attention, the Total Team felt they needed to change consumer awareness, making them aware that hidden problems such as gum disease, gingivitis, and plaque were bigger threats to their well-being as they got older than cavity protection. As their approach to selling Total took hold, the team hit on the "long-lasting protection" theme as the new formula's unique selling proposition and the sales campaign began to take shape from there.

Television advertising came only after preparing the industry's gatekeepers, namely dentists. Colgate dispatched, via overnight courier, 30 million samples of Total to dentists' offices around the country. They spent $20 million informing dentists of the product's therapeutic benefits, answering their questions, informing them of how Colgate developers had relied on leading dental schools to discover a way to bond Triclosan to teeth and how it was clinically proven to fight gingivitis. It was the only paste cleared to make such claims by the FDA.

That done, the team turned its attention to the distribution channel. "The whole process for Total was different," recalls Lou Mignone, vice president of U.S. sales. "We did pre-planning with senior merchandising executives at the major retailers and worked with them on timing the introduction and getting the product to market as efficiently as possible."

The team also coordinated the distribution process for the trade, bypassing warehouses and sending individual cases to stores, which ensured all retailers had their shipments within a week, versus the usual five to eight weeks. Then and only then did the team turn to television. One television spot showed a hurried young executive going through his busy day, as the sound of brushing follows him everywhere. "Now there's a toothpaste so advanced," observed the voiceover, "it even works when you're not brushing."

In our interview with the product's champion, Jack Haber described a moment when he was sure that Team Total had come up with not only a breakthrough product but a breakthrough selling strategy as well. "At a dinner the night before a big sales meeting, before any speeches were given, everyone was so happy and so pumped we could have concluded the meeting then. I never saw such electricity in a room before and it translated because the marketing group had it, sales had it, R&D had it, buyers had it, retailers had it, and I just knew then that in a matter of a few weeks, consumers would have it too. We were all celebrating."

Developing Your 21st Century Approach to Selling New Ideas

As Team Total surely knows, discovery and invention of a new product or service are not nearly enough. To derive growth from innovation, you have to build the buy-in for your idea, sometimes one customer at a time. You have to go out and knock on doors, and find people who can use your product. These days, as computer mouse inventor Douglas Engelbart put it, the biggest challenge isn't how to innovate a better mousetrap, it's how to get people to adopt your better mousetrap. Here are some key questions to ponder as you reflect on the ideas in this chapter.

1. How good an evangelist are you? How have your persuasive skills and abilities been improving over the past, say, five years? How quickly and effectively do you identify the benefits and the value-added to be derived by the customer? And to your subordinates, channel partners, and others on the management team?

2. How effective has your firm been in recent years in launching products, services, and internal changes that require employee

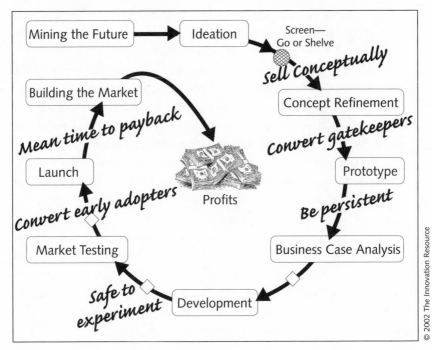

Figure 7   Idea-to-Implementation in Your Company   Selling ideas internally and externally is important at every stage.

buy-in? What learning needed to take place? What assumptions proved invalid and what will you do differently next time?

3. Thinking about an idea you had recently, who were the stakeholders you needed to convince to accept your idea? How effective were you in utilizing the skills outlined in this chapter?

4. How does the sharing of best practices take place in your company in this all-important arena of selling new ideas? Are teams giving enough attention to this final, vital phase that is so critical to successful innovation?

There's no question that successfully selling new ideas is the essential, capstone skill of innovation-adept companies and idea champions. In the public's imagination, the act of selling often gets confused with hucksterism, manipulation, and unsavory practices. But as every sales and marketing professional knows, nothing happens until the sale is made, the customer hands over his or her hard-earned money and buys your new idea that good things start happening.

After you've pondered the questions posed above and throughout this chapter, consider this: It's often the front-end of innovation that is considered fuzzy. But after working with numerous companies to improve their innovation processes, I often find that the real fuzziness lies at this, the back end of the process, and it needs major revamping such that selling ideas becomes a stepping stone rather than a stumbling block to driving growth.

And with that, let's move to the final chapter, which has to do with where to get started in implementing the ideas this book has discussed. ◄

CHAPTER 10

Taking Action in Your Firm

Innovation is ultimately not an act of intellect but of will.

—Joseph Schumpeter

Having read this far, it is safe to assume that you are someone deeply involved in or concerned about the future of your firm. And having read all about what the Innovation Vanguard firms are doing, and having jotted down your own ideas as to how to best develop an innovation process for your firm, you now face a choice—whether you will act on your ideas or whether you'll let your good intentions lapse.

The choice is what you will do with the ideas you've gained from investing your time in reading this book. It could easily be that the forward progress of your firm rests on what you decide to do at this point.

You could chose to file your notes away in a folder marked "someday." But that wouldn't help you and your firm to address the Growth Gap we talked about in Chapter 1.

Fact is, no business consciously sets out to manage the past, to allow growth to lapse. No leader sets out to let this happen. Instead, it happens gradually. The world continues to change. Customers' needs continue to change. The business keeps on serving up yesterday's ideas . . . until it's too late.

On the other hand, you could decide to act on your intentions and on the ideas you hatched as you read through this book and developed your 21st Century Innovation Blueprint. The question is, where should you start to take action, how do you gain support for your beliefs, and what exactly should you do?

Acting on Your Ideas

Recall that in each of the Vanguard firms we reported on, *somebody somewhere did something to get things going.* Hark back to our first case example: At Citigroup it was Victor Menezes, then CEO of Citibank, who saw the potential to derive serious growth from an improved innovation approach. In other companies, it was a divisional manager (Royal Dutch/Shell) or a general manager (Bristol-Myers Squibb) who first took action, built the buy-in, demonstrated measurable results, and eventually brought the entire company onboard.

Whether you're the CEO, a mid-level manager, a project manager or line executive, or a passionate individual contributor, determines how you will proceed. But your position, assuming that you're not the CEO, shouldn't dissuade you from taking action. You can build support for looking at new ideas to jump-start innovation in your firm no matter what your title is.

If you're an individual contributor, you can pick up the phone and call some of the people we've written about in these pages and ask them for their ideas. You can tap the resources listed in the Source Notes & Resources at the end of this book, and attend the conferences listed where you'll be able to interact with others who are currently or have already done what you're trying to do.

In so doing, you'll be able to further polish the first draft of your proposed innovation strategy. At the same time, you'll want to start "talking up" what other firms are doing in the Innovation Movement, planting seeds in people's minds. In other words, start putting innovation on the agenda, every agenda you can. Start being a quiet evangelist for change and a subtle educator on the subject.

Next, identify others in your organization who have an interest in the topic. Find out what they know, what they are reading, what their thinking is on the field, and begin the process of bringing them up to speed on what you're thinking. Listen to their insights and ideas and feed back to them that their ideas may not be so far-fetched after all; then tell them about the companies in this book.

What you're after is a core team of people who believe, as you do, that "there's got to be a better way" to do innovation, and that growth can be the result. To find your core team, write up the notes you've jotted down while reading this book, polish them a bit, and share them with anybody you talk with inside the firm who shows genuine interest.

Please do not call this document a manifesto, and fight the tendency to suggest that those in upper management "don't get it." While some of our colleagues in the Innovation Movement advocate writing manifestos and charging the gates of administrator-caretaker leaders, we have seen that such rhetoric is counterproductive to building the buy-in for change. Research with Innovation Vanguard companies suggests that the politics of inclusion and quiet, persistent coalition-building works far better.

Why? Because it brings everybody along, doesn't create enemies in the future, and stresses the benefits everyone in the company will enjoy when these suggestions for improvement are implemented. Innovation, like Total Quality Management 20 years ago, is a movement. Most companies judge their quality initiatives to be fairly successful, and they are proud of the results.

On the other hand, most companies were dissatisfied with their attempts at reengineering. The difference? The Quality Movement understood the need to involve everybody—from the shop floor to the executive suites. The Reengineering Movement did not. The advocates of reengineering thought they could design individual processes in a company, and achieve dramatic cost-savings. Instead they created massive distrust and alienation because people felt threatened. Would they have a job at the end of all the chaos? What was the benefit to the individual? The Innovation Vanguard companies have taken to heart the necessity that wide participation and demystification of any change effort are necessary for success.

Mapping Out an Innovation Initiative

After you've gained support from others in the organization who see the need for an improved approach to innovation, you're ready to map out an innovation initiative. You and a core team of people will want to prepare an innovation initiative that addresses each of the following key areas:

Objectives

What is the present growth rate of your firm and how does that compare with your overall industry? What does your company's growth rate need to be to meet stakeholder requirements?

Is There a Growth Gap in Your Company?

What is the state of innovation adeptness in your firm? What breakthrough ideas have you introduced in the past five years? How promising are the ideas in your current pipeline?

Leadership and Metrics

1. How do you intend to embed innovation in your organization?

2. What are the desired outcomes of an innovation initiative?

3. What structural/leadership barriers currently exist that must change if innovation is to become a company wide priority and an effective process?

4. How must your measurement systems be changed to ensure senior management commitment and attention be paid to innovation long after the initiative has been launched?

5. Who will be in charge of designing and launching an Innovation Initiative?

Culture

1. What are the desired values and behaviors you want to encourage?

2. How will you reward and recognize innovative behavior?

3. How will the initiative be communicated, and what training will

be available to assist people in mastering new ways of approaching their work?

4. What continual reinforcement process will be in place to support an innovative culture?

Idea Management

1. How effective is your current system of soliciting, gathering, and implementing ideas from all employees, and all parts of the organization?

2. How will this system need to be redesigned or improved to ensure that good ideas don't get lost?

3. After reviewing the eight idea management models in Chapter 4, which model seems to make the most sense for your firm? In what ways will you need to customize your model?

Future-Mining/Ideation Capabilities

1. How effectively is your firm scanning and monitoring the sources of future opportunity?

2. In what ways are you and your colleagues coming together to assault industry assumptions and examine the opportunities in emerging changes?

3. How could you become more effective in identifying the unarticulated needs of present customers, and potential new customer groups?

4. What new methods might you adopt and adapt from other companies to strengthen your processes in identifying threats and possible innovations?

5. How are you identifying new strategy innovations?

Responsibilities and Timeline

1. Define who will be responsible for the design and implementation of your innovation initiative, and what the deliverables will be.

2. Review the initiative with your CEO. Get commitment and clearly agree on how it ties to your firm's overall company strategy.

3. Review the initiative with individual members of the executive committee and define how the initiative needs to be modified for their areas of responsibility. (Get their buy-in to the initiative.)

4. Review the initiative with the entire executive committee as a group.

5. Agree on feedback mechanism from each area regarding progress toward the goals.

6. Agree on a company-wide roll-out plan.

7. Roll it out, starting with the CEO. An innovation initiative has to start from the top.

Deciding Where to Start

As a consultant, the question I most often get is, where do we start to upgrade our innovation process? My answer is that it depends on a number of factors, from your industry's clockspeed to your present culture and growth targets. But at the risk of painting with too broad a brush, I find most companies can best start by rethinking and redesigning their idea management systems. As we said at the beginning of this book, beyond a seldom-used suggestion box, most companies have allowed their methods of encouraging, nurturing, and acting on employee suggestions to languish. So consider starting there.

When idea management systems are designed by a cross-functional group of people, they have the best chance of acceptance. Moreover, in the act of designing and implementing a new and improved system, you will effectively accomplish other objectives as well. You'll be putting innovation on the agenda. You'll be discussing and learning about the discipline of innovation. You'll inevitably be looking at innovation, not as the function and purview of only certain departments, but of the total enterprise, and every department, division, and person in it.

You'll be taking steps that just possibly will lead to an even deeper and more fundamental transforming of your firm's future.

You'll inevitably be called to discuss the ideas you'll receive when you publicly ask people to contribute them. And if you're like most companies, you'll be pleasantly surprised that there are so many truly good ideas out there—that you might not have even heard about! So, start your Innovation Initiative by focusing on how much more effectively you can solicit and reward and develop and act on the ideas that are in your organization.

In doing so, you'll be joining others in the Innovation Movement from around the globe who are reshaping their firms for 21st century success. We constantly hear from these individuals, and the common theme is simply this: They believe that innovation is one of the most exciting things they've ever worked on in their careers.

My hope is that, as you embark upon your own journey, that you will soon agree, and I wish you great success!

Acknowledgments

Although the Innovation Movement this book describes is recent, it builds upon the work of thinkers and practitioners who have plowed these fields for decades. Clearly, to quote Sir Isaac Newton, "I have stood on the shoulders of giants" in writing this book.

Closer to home, I acknowledge the contributions and support of my wife, Carolyn, to whom this book is dedicated, and my daughter, Cara Rose. It is not easy living with someone whose career takes him away as much as mine, and, to add insult to injury, it was necessary for me to go to the office on Saturdays for these past three years. I look forward to returning to a normal life, and thank both of you for enabling me to pursue this project to completion.

I also wish to thank my brother, Bart Tucker, a senior consultant with The Innovation Resource, for his belief in and constant support of this project. Throughout, Bart was always there, lending a hand, making suggestions, and always encouraging us to keep going.

Joel Gustafson was also an early supporter and sounding board for the ideas in this book, and an enthusiastic researcher, as was Dorothy Pedersen. A special debt of gratitude to Julia Mariani, who manages my speaking schedule and media appearances, for her many hours spent improving this manuscript and establishing contact with the Vanguard companies.

Our colleagues and friends at Citigroup deserve special acknowledgement especially Victor Menezes, Senior Vice Chairman, for his vision in launching an innovation initiative in what was until recently called the Emerging Markets Division; Jorge Bermudez, now CEO of Citibank Latin America, for serving as founding leader of the initiative, and Claus Friis, who has managed the initiative day to day from its inception. Michael Contreras, EVP, Global Relationship Bank head, was an early and enthusiastic advocate of innovation, as were Elcio Pereira and Alexis Goncalves in Latin America, and Renzo Viegas and Vicki DeSouza in Asia Pacific.

To my colleagues at Gold Coast and to all of those who read and commented on the manuscript, a hearty thank you: Linda S. Mayer, Mavis Wilson, Jane Haubrich Casperson, Douglas Hammer, Katherine Holt, Angela Wagner, Dan Burrus, Mark Sanborn, Charles Prather, Michael LeBoeuf, Gordon Burgett, Dan Poynter, Dennis Black, and Art Fry.

And finally, to our new friends at Berrett-Koehler, and especially to Steven Piersanti, publisher, thank you for your professionalism, dedication, and integrity—we look forward to a long and productive relationship.

Source Notes
and Resources

Author's Note: In addition to citing the source for stories and direct quotes used in this book, I've also included relevant resources you may wish to tap.

For the latest URLs on various educational products and groups listed here, please visit our website at: www.innovationresource.com

Introduction
Page 1 The PricewaterhouseCoopers survey is titled *Innovation & Growth: A Global Perspective*, by Trevor Davis. It was privately published but is available for purchase.

2 The Arthur D. Little survey is titled *Findings of the Arthur D. Little Global Survey on Innovation*. Privately published, it is available for purchase from A. D. Little.

4 Journalist John Grossman's inside account of the ideation session appeared in the cover story, "Jump Start Your Business," *Inc. Magazine*, May 1997.

6 Insights into AT&T's Opportunity Discovery Department came from a presentation by Amy Muller, director of corporate strategy and business development at AT&T, at the Institute for International Research conference *Strategic Innovation: Inspiration, Action, & Results*, November 1999.

7 Nearly two-thirds of managers said their companies don't use even half their brainpower: "Think About It: Your Brainpower May

Be Vastly Underused on the Job," *Wall Street Journal*, February 11, 1997.

Chapter 1: 21st Century Innovation

13 "Innovation is vital to our future," Victor Menezes' quote is from his speech to the Citibank Latin America Region's Revenue Momentum Workshop, December 2001, and is used with permission.

14 The Corporate Strategy Board study of 3,700 companies was summarized in "The Growth Imperative," by Jude T. Rich, *Journal of Business Strategy*, March/April 1999.

15 Just 23 percent of acquisitions earn their cost of capital; the McKinsey study was summarized in "Growing Your Company: Five Ways to Do It Right," by Ronald Henkoff, *Fortune*, November 25, 1996. Also see "How Big Companies Grow," *Harvard Management Update*, May 1999.

16 The landmark study conducted by PricewaterhouseCoopers refers to the study previously cited.

16 Medtronic typically derives 70 percent of revenues from products less than two years old; and other statistics were compiled from press reports and interviews with company officials.

Of course, mere turnover of products alone is not the sole measure. Otherwise, auto manufacturers, book publishers, and others with 100 percent turnover of their products annually would all be growth champions. Vanguard companies strive to produce distinct offerings as well as genuine improvements.

17 Survey findings from the Industrial Research Institute were published in "The Boom in Industry Research," *Science & Technology*, Summer 2000.

18 "Innovation is critical to my company's survival . . ." Proprietary research conducted under the direction of Jeff Mauzy of The Synectics Corporation, Fairfax, Virginia, 1993.

18 A. D. Little survey previously cited.

28 The major study of radical innovations, conducted by a team of researchers at Rensselaer Polytechnic Institute, was reported in "Getting to Eureka: Researchers Are Tracking How Breakthroughs Are Made," *Business Week*, November 10, 1997. See also the important book *Radical Innovation: How Mature Companies Can Outsmart Upstarts*, by Richard Leifer, Mark Rice, et al. Harvard Business School Press, Boston, 2000.

29 Findings of the Arthur D. Little *Global Survey on Innovation*, previously cited.

31 The story of Citigroup's new approach to innovation was gleaned from extensive interviews with company officials and the author's involvement as a consultant and presenter during the design and rollout of the Global Innovation Initiative.

Chapter 2: Leading Innovation

37 "What is striking is not just the number of CEOs getting the boot": "The CEO Trap", *Business Week*, December 11, 2000.

38 John McCoy was long touted as a visionary: See "You Can't Take Vision to the Bank," by Martin Mayer, *Wall Street Journal*, December 28, 1999.

44 "We're going to become a five billion dollar organization": John Fiedler's quote is from "Want Innovation: Oil the Machine, and Water the Garden," by Thomas A. Stewart, *Fortune*, 2000.

44 "Peter always had straightforward objectives for management": Progressive Insurance senior vice president Alan Bauer's quote is from an interview with the author.

44 The Borg-Warner case study was compiled from interviews with Simon Spencer, B-W's Innovation Champion, and David Sutherland, president of Business Innovation Consortium, a consulting firm.

46 The EDS case study was compiled from extensive interviews with Melinda Lockhart, manager of EDS Innovates, and from company documents.

48 "A lot of times the best marketing ideas don't come from marketing." Jon Letzler's comments from an interview with the author.

54 "Let's say you pay on division profit sharing": Paul Guehler's comments are from an interview with the author.

55 "You stupid old geezer": This paraphrase of a familiar story is most often told by philosopher and proponent of intrinsic rewards,

Alfie Kohn. See "Unrewarding Rewards," by A. J. Vogl, *Across the Board*, January 1994.

Chapter 3: Creating the Culture

58 Before its collapse and bankruptcy, Enron's internal environment was most often described by business writers, Wall Street analysts, and consultants as the very model of an innovative culture. After the fall, further revelations about the culture revealed an "unrelenting stress on growth and an absence of controls" that "helped push execs into unethical behavior" to meet targets. See for example, "The Environment Was Ripe for Abuse," by John A. Byrne, *Business Week*, February 25, 2002.

58 "I recall an instructor whose way of checking to see": Mary Jean Ryan's quote is from her essay, "Driving Out Fear: One CEO's Personal Journey, *Healthcare Forum Journal*, July/August 1996.

59 "The very cultural traits that made these companies successful may preclude their ability": see Charlan Jeanne Nemeth's article "Managing Innovation: When Less is More," *California Management Review*, Fall 1997.

60 "After 10–15 years of these programs, most have been terminated": see the report, "The Future of Corporate Innovation Centers," by Jack Hipple, and produced under the auspices of the Association of Managers for Innovation, available via their website. See www.innovationresource.com for current contact information.

61 The story of Post-it® Notes has been told in numerous places; see for example *Breakthroughs: How the Vision and Drive of Innovators in 16 Companies Created Commercial Breakthroughs That Swept the World*, by P. Panganath Nayak and John M. Ketteringham, Rawson Associates, New York, 1986.

62 "We had a difficult time building the buy-in for Post-it Notes": See "Interviews with Innovators," *Fast Company*, April 2000.

65 Diagnosing and objectively understanding your organization or work group's barriers to innovation is an important first step toward improvement. There are various assessment tools and benchmarking surveys available—some are free for the downloading, others are proprietary and available only in the context of a consultative project. For a list of the climate surveys we recommend, visit

www.innovationresource.com

66 Innovation Best Practices Survey Report produced jointly by Innovation Network and Global Best Practices, privately published.

66 Knowledge workers receive 52 phone interruptions, 36 e-mails: These totals were contained in the article "Message Overload Taking Toll on Workers," by Kirsten Grimsley, *The Washington Post*, May 20, 1998.

67 "Room Sealed by Order of 'No Meeting Day' Police," see "Memo to Staff: Stop Working," by Joann S. Lublin, *Wall Street Journal*, July 6, 2000.

68 3M's policy of 15 percent free time "is not a written rule": Paul Guehler's comments are from an interview with the author.

69 "Sometimes the ideas compete with something the company is already doing": Dr. Glen Nelson's comments are from interviews with the author.

71 "Pat Farrah is just a wild man": This former executive's comments appeared in "A Free Spirit Energizes Home Depot," by James R. Hagerty, *Wall Street Journal*, April 11, 2000.

71 "When people are faced with a majority of others who agree": Charlan Jeanne Nemeth's quote is from her article "Managing Innovation: When Less Is More," *California Management Review*, Fall 1997.

72 Michael Kirton's 33 item survey, the KAI Inventory, is used to assess an individual's preferred creativity style. Only certified practitioners may administer it. You will find resources at:

www.bottomlineinnovation.com

www.kaicentre.com

http://web.indstate.edu/soe/blumberg/KAI.html

Check these sites if you want to find a certified practitioner or to explore certification for yourself.

73 "The people bring high value to any business"; Charles Prather's comments are from interviews with the author.

73 Innovation Wizard is a web-based resource created by the InnovationNetwork that offers organizations everything they need to build and sustain an innovation competency: idea stimulators, best practices, a complete model of innovation, articles, and reports, as well as a powerful series of "5-minute Workshops" that deliver practical tools and techniques as needed. It's user-friendly graphic environment engages people in the process of "generating and implementing new ideas that create value." For more information:

mailto.innovationwizard@thinksmart.com
http://www.thinksmart.com.

74 Starbucks' popular Frappuccino drink's origins were reported in "Ground-Level Innovation," *Harvard Management Update*, August 2000.

76 "You can't have a leaderless matrix because then the team wanders": Bill Steere's comments are from "Mothers of Invention," *Chief Executive*, July–August 1996.

76 "We have yet to find a success that happened without a strong champion": Gifford Pinchot's comments are from his book, *Intrapreneuring: Why You Don't Have to Leave the Corporation to Become an Entrepreneur*, Harper & Row, New York, 1985.

77 Findings from the 3M team's efforts to identify signs of innovative potential were reported in the book, *The 3M Way to Innovation: Balancing People and Profit*, by Ernest Gundling, Kodansha International, Tokyo, Japan, 2000.

Chapter 4: Empowering the Idea Management Process

79 "The old Borg-Warner would have said you can't organize the innovation process": author interview with Simon Spencer, B-W Innovation Champion.

79 The Monday Morning Wake Up Brain e-zine is available free of charge to members and nonmembers of The Innovation Network. See www.innovationresource.com for details on how to register.

80 "We were not about to abandon our product development processes": Comments from Robert Goss, Whirlpool Corporation's innovation leader, are from an interview with the author.

81 The Kathryn Kridel anecdote was originally recorded in the book, *Corporate Creativity: How Innovation and Improvement Actually*

Happen, by Alan G. Robinson and Sam Stern, Berrett-Koehler Publishers, San Francisco, 1997.

81 "The [suggestion] systems coming out now are computerized, professionally managed and have real incentives": John Holland, former president of the Employee Involvement Association, was quoted from an interview with the author.

84 Our study of Dana Corporation's continuous improvement program was made possible by interviews with Gary Corigan, corporate communications, and from various articles. See especially: "How to Harness Gray Matter," by Richard Teitelbaum, *Fortune*, June 9, 1997.

86 "We believe our people doing the job are the true experts in their area": Joseph M. Magliochetti, Dana chairman, was quoted from an interview with the author.

86 "We have an open door policy that any employee": Melinda Lockhart, global innovation manager at EDS, was quoted from interviews with the author.

86 Information on Disney's Gong Shows is from "A Mickey Mouse Way to Run Companies," by Anne Fisher, *Fortune*, March 29, 1999, and from *The Disney Way*, by Bill Capodagli and Lynn Jackson, McGraw-Hill, New York, 1998.

86 Disney chairman Michael Eisner's book is *Work in Progress*, with Tony Schwartz, Random House, New York, 1998.

87 Ailsa Petchey's story is recounted in "Reinvent Your Company: 10 Rules for Making Billion-dollar Business Ideas Bubble Up From Below," an excerpt of Gary Hamel's book, *Leading the Revolution*, in *Fortune*, June 12, 2000.

87 Procter & Gamble's new venture approach is the subject of Harvard Business School case study 9-897-088, "Corporate New Ventures at P&G," and author interviews with Craig Wynett, innovation chief at P&G.

88 Nortel's short-lived experiment with phantom stock was reported in "Using the Net for Brainstorming," by Marcia Stepanek, *Business Week*, December 13, 1999.

88 EDS's case study was reported based on extensive interviews with Melinda Lockhart, innovation maven, and company documents.

90 Xerox's sale of PARC was reported in "Xerox to Spin Off Research Center," by Karen Kaplan, *Los Angeles Times*, December 12, 2001.

90 Appleton Paper's Growth Opportunities (GO) program is spearheaded by Dennis Hultgren, and this case study is based on interviews by the author.

94 "We had this internal market of people we weren't tapping": Nancy Snyder, Whirlpool's vice president of strategic competency creation, was quoted in "Recipe for Growth," by Fara Warner, *Fast Company*, October 2001.

95 Case study of Citigroup's Catalyst Approach to innovation was compiled by interviews with numerous Citibankers and the author's involvement in the Global Innovation Initiative.

Chapter 5: Mining the Future

105 "We get 50 proposals a year": Quotes from Dave Austgen, Shell Chemical's GameChanger leader, are from interviews with the author.

106 The front end of innovation appears to represent the greatest area of weakness": This quote is from a research project that collectively determined a theoretical construct for the Fuzzy Front End of
innovation. See the article summarizing the reaearch, "Providing Clarity and a Common Language to the 'Fuzzy Front End,'" by Peter Koen, Robin Karol, et al., *Journal of the Industrial Research Institute*, Spring 2001.

107 How Progressive made lemonade from a regulatory lemon: details are from "Progressive Makes Big Claims," by Chuck Salter, *Fast Company*, November 1998.

108 See *Winning the Innovation Game*, by Denis Waitley and Robert B. Tucker, Fleming H. Revell, Englewood, New Jersey, 1986.

110 The author's interview with Frederick Smith, founder and chairman of Federal Express, appeared in "The Man Who Created Overnight Delivery Says You Absolutely, Positively Have to Innovate—If Only to Survive," *Inc. Magazine*, October 1986.

111 BMW Group's Future Scan System was reported from interviews with company officials in Palo Alto, and David Sutherland, innovation consultant to BMW and founder of Business Innovation Consortium, Baltimore, Maryland.

113 "Our company works best when we continue to ask questions": Maxie Carpenter's quote is from "Always Reinventing . . . Always: Wal-Mart Has Maintained a Staggering Growth Pace Thanks Largely to Its Commitment to Trying New Things," by Lois Flowers, *Life@Work Journal*, Spring 1999.

114 "We have literally turned the pyramid upside down": Lewis L. Edelheit's comments are from "GE's R&D Strategy: Be Vital," *Research-Technology Management*, March/April 1998.

115 See "First to Market, First to Fail: Real Causes of Enduring Market Leadership," by Gerard J. Tellis and Peter N. Golder, *Sloan Management Review*, Winter 1996.

119 This section on first mover advantages and disadvantages was greatly enhanced by several discussions with Joe Gilbert, Ph.D., professor of business administration at the University of Nevada, Las Vegas, a leading expert in this area of innovation. See his definitive article, "Innovation Timing Advantages: From Economic Theory to Strategic Application," *Journal of Engineering and Technology Management*," Spring,1996.

120 *Business Week*'s estimate of marketing expenditures for Miller Lite were reported by Tellis and Golder, previously cited.

121 "Begin with the end in mind": Steven R. Covey's book is *The Seven Habits of Highly Effective People*, Simon & Schuster, New York, 1989.

Chapter 6: Fortifying the Idea Factory

123 "Innovation isn't just a front-end activity": The quote from Nancy Eicher, is from "Innovation DNA: A Good Idea Isn't Enough. It has to Create Value," by Ruth Ann Hattori and Joyce Wycoff, *Training & Development*, January 2002.

123 Thanks to Mark Rice, Ph.D., professor at Rensselaer, for interpreting and elaborating on this research. Also see the book *Radical*

Innovation: How Mature Companies Can Outsmart Upstarts, by Richard Leifer, Mark Rice, et al. Harvard Business School Press, Boston, 2000.

127 "I was really proud of everybody and the ideas submitted": Marsha MacArthur, is quoted from an interview with the author, and company documents.

127 Additional information on the Bristol-Myers Squibb (BMS) program is available from Imaginatik, a Boston-based software company. Its Idea Central product, adopted by BMS and other companies, is an idea management application "designed to focus the creative brainpower of employees and extended enterprise partners to generate business-focused ideas, develop those ideas, and then evaluate and select the best concepts for implementation or further development."

128 The study of 123 firms concluding that new products are most often initiated by ideas from customers is reported in "The Impact of Product Innovativeness on Performance," by E. J. Kleinschmidt and Robert J. Cooper, *Journal of Product Innovation Management* 8, no. 4 (1991).

128 Information about BMW's Virtual Innovation Agency is available on the automaker's website.

129 "The preferences were probably there for years": Bruce Karatz's quote is from "Surprise! A Home Builder (Finally) Surveys Buyers," *Wall Street Journal*, June 5, 1998.

130 Automakers aren't the only ones using ethnography as a way of getting a jump on what consumers will want next. See, for example, "Consumers in the Mist: Mad Ave.'s Anthropologists Are Unearthing Our Secrets," by Gerry Khermouch, *Business Week*, February 26, 2001.

130 The PT Cruiser design team's use of archetype research methods pioneered by G. Clotaire Rapaille are reported in "But How Does It Make You Feel?" by Jeffrey Ball, *Wall Street Journal*, May 3, 1999.

132 My understanding of the unarticulated needs of customers was enhanced by "Speed: Linking Innovation, Process, and Time to Market," a Conference Board Report researched and written by Marilyn Zuckerman Michaels, available from The Conference

Board. See www.innovationservice.com for information on obtaining this report.

132 "First, I ask customers about their experience with services like ours": David Pottruck, is quoted from an excerpt of his book, *Clicks and Mortar: Passion Driven Growth in an Internet Driven World*, by Pottruck, with Terry Pearce, Jossey-Bass, San Francisco, 2000.

135 "Hearing heart murmurs . . . was becoming increasingly difficult": Jay Mazelsky's comments are from "Listen Up: You Can't Learn What Your Customers Want If You Don't Know How to Listen to Them," by Rekha Balu, *Fast Company*, May 2000.

135 "If you have any new ideas or technologies": This senior executive's quotes and insights are from an interview with the author. The executive asked not to be identified based on a directive from the company's communications department.

136 Research by my company, The Innovation Resource, on behalf of a leading battery-maker, enabled us to seek out firms with stellar relationships with their suppliers. These guidelines are a summary of our findings, based on interviews with companies in 1999.

138 "Respect the newborns, tomorrow we'll strangle them": Ideation specialist Doug Hall's quote, as well as insights into his methods, are from "Jump Start Your Business," by John Grossman, *Inc. Magazine*, May 1997. While Doug Hall is a leader in this burgeoning field, there are a number of others. Check out our list at:
www.innovationresource.com

139 "We've learned from the best": the quote from Robin Karol, is from an interview with the author.

Chapter 7: Producing Powerful Products

143 "People don't pay for technology": Dean Kamen's quote is from an interview with the author for the book, *Winning the Innovation Game*, by Denis Waitley and Robert B. Tucker, Fleming Revel, Englewood, New Jersey, 1986.

144 Kuczmarski & Associates' study of 209 company practices is titled "The K&A Winning New Product and Service Practices Study," March 2000. www.kuczmarski.com

151 For further information on Robert G. Cooper's stage-gate approach, see, "How to Launch a New Product Successfully," by Robert G. Cooper, *CMA Magazine*, October 1995.

152 While the gated approach to new products has gained tremendous popularity, it is by no means the only approach. See, for example, *The Focused Innovation Technique*, and the workbook, *Developing New Product Concepts*, by Chris Miller, founder and president of Innovation Focus, Lancaster, PA. www.innovationfocus.com

152 See also *The PDMA Toolbook for New Product Development*, which can be purchased online. See the Product Development Management Association's website for more information on the conferences and other publications of this group.

153 "What you end up with is rarely what you started with": Gary Lynn's comments are from "Innovation Strategies Under Uncertainty: A Contingency Approach for New Product Development," by Gary S. Lynn and Ali E. Akgun, *Engineering Management Journal*, September 1998. Professor Lynn was interviewed by the author.

155 "'Shared space' is the dominant medium for collaboration": Michael Schrage's comments are from "The Path to Innovation: MIT's Michael Schrage Explains How Corporate Culture Contributes to Innovation in the Age of the Internet," by Kim Austin Peterson, *IQ Magazine* (Cisco), undated article.

156 "This is when we started to think, 'maybe we've got something here'": Frank Nekic's comments, as well as Doug Ringger's are from an interview with the author.

Chapter 8: Generating Growth Strategies

163 "Interesting and innovative ideas do not a business make": Michael Schrage's quote is from "The Path to Innovation: MIT's Michael Schrage Explains How Corporate Culture Contributes to Innovation in the Age of the Internet," by Kim Austin Peterson, *IQ Magazine* (Cisco), undated article.

165 "Category killers will be a diminishing force": Richard W. Latella's quote is from "Category Killers Go From Lethal to Lame in the Space of a Decade," by William M. Bulkeley, *Wall Street Journal*, March 9, 2000.

165 Readers interested in pursuing their study of strategy innovation might well start with a definitive article called, "Strategy, Value Innovation, and the Knowledge Economy," by W. Chan Kim and Renee Mauborgne, *Sloan Management Review*, Spring 1999. See also their article "Creating New Market Space," *Harvard Business Review*, January/February 1999.

165 The case study of the evolution of Tyson Foods is based on press articles, excellent assistance from Archie Schaffer of Tyson's public relations office, and interviews with Don Tyson, former chairman of the company.

167 See "DirecTV Beats Forecasts, Cuts Hughes' Loss," *Los Angeles Times*, January 17, 2001.

171 "There's a whole movement taking place from fix-me dentistry to transform-me dentistry": see "Seeing Green in Pearly Whites: Teeth Whitening Has Grown into a $600 Million Industry," by Marc Ballon, *Los Angeles Times*, October 20, 1999.

172 "It was a wake-up call": Peter Lewis' quote is from "Progressive Makes Big Claims," by Chuck Salter, *Fast Company*, November 1998.

Chapter 9: Selling New Ideas

175 "Sure, innovation is critical, but": Doug Engelbart's quote is from "Interviews with Innovators," *Fast Company*, April 2000.

177 The Consumer Electronics Association estimate of new product introductions is from "Deluge of Electronic Goodies Overloads Customers' Circuits," by P. J. Huffstutter, *Los Angeles Times*, January 6, 2001.

178 Computer manufacturers are struggling to deliver meaningful-enough innovation, see "As More Buyers Suffer From Upgrade Fatigue, PC Sales Are Falling," by Gary McWilliams, *Wall Street Journal*, August 24, 2001.

182 For details see, "Whirlpool and P&G Hope to Alter Consumer Habits," by Julian E. Barnes, *New York Times*, March 16, 2001.

182 Information about the slowness of advertisers to accept *USA Today* is from a Harvard Case Study of the newspaper, by Hilary Weston under the supervision of professor Robert Simons, 1990.

182 For background information on Webvan, see "Will Webvan Ever Find a Better Way to Bring Home the Bacon?" by Kara Swisher, *Wall Street Journal*, October 2, 2000.

185 "I'd say, 'this machine will do this and this'": Tom Lambert's quote is from "Innovation Strategies Under Uncertainty," by Lynn and Akgun, previously cited.

186 "We had it tested for strength and stiffness": Stephanie Kwolek, Kevlar's co-inventor, was quoted in "Interviews with Innovators," *Fast Company*, April 2000.

189 "Haber is a discreetly ponytailed mensch": See "Jack Haber: Getting Totaled," by Christine Bittar, *Brandweek*, October 12, 1998.

189 The case study of Colgate's Total is based on author interviews with Jack Haber, numerous published accounts, and company documents.

Chapter 10: Taking Action in Your Firm

199 A special thanks to Linda S. Mayer, senior vice president marketing and product development at Moen Incorporated, for her suggestions on taking action to implement the ideas and strategies in this book.

Index

About the Author

Robert B. Tucker is an internationally recognized leader in the field of innovation. Formerly an adjunct professor at the University of California, Los Angeles, Tucker has been studying innovators and innovative companies since 1981.

His pioneering research in interviewing over 50 leading American innovators was published in the book *Winning the Innovation Game* in 1986. Since then, he has continued to publish widely on the subject, including his international bestseller, *Managing the Future: 10 Driving Forces of Change for the New Century*, which has been translated into 13 languages.

As one of the thought leaders in the growing Innovation Movement, Tucker is a frequent contributor to business periodicals such as *Journal of Business Strategy* and *Strategy & Leadership*. He has appeared on CNBC, CBS News, and was a featured guest on the PBS series, *Taking the Lead*.

As president of The Innovation Resource, a research and innovation consulting firm, Tucker is a much sought after speaker at conferences and company convocations. Clients range from Fortune 500 companies to national and international trade associations. He has been a consultant to Taiwan's Economic Development Ministry, and the Japan Marketing Association, and he has assisted numerous organizations throughout the world in improving their approach to innovation.

To communicate with Robert Tucker, to schedule a speaking or consulting engagement, or for more information about his programs and audio and video products and web-based training opportunities, contact:

The Innovation Resource
100 North Hope Avenue, Suite 19
Santa Barbara, California 93110
U. S. A.

Tel (805) 682-1012
Fax (805) 682-8960
Web: www.innovationresource.com
E-mail info@innovationresource.com

Berrett-Koehler Publishers

Berrett-Koehler is an independent publisher of books, periodicals, and other publications at the leading edge of new thinking and innovative practice on work, business, management, leadership, stewardship, career development, human resources, entrepreneurship, and global sustainability.

Since the company's founding in 1992, we have been committed to supporting the movement toward a more enlightened world of work by publishing books, periodicals, and other publications that help us to integrate our values with our work and work lives, and to create more humane and effective organizations.

We have chosen to focus on the areas of work, business, and organizations, because these are central elements in many people's lives today. Furthermore, the work world is going through tumultuous changes, from the decline of job security to the rise of new structures for organizing people and work. We believe that change is needed at all levels—individual, organizational, community, and global—and our publications address each of these levels.

We seek to create new lenses for understanding organizations, to legitimize topics that people care deeply about but that current business orthodoxy censors or considers secondary to bottom-line concerns, and to uncover new meaning, means, and ends for our work and work lives.

See next pages for other publications from Berrett-Koehler Publishers

Berrett-Koehler Publishers
PO Box 565, Williston, VT 05495-9900
Call toll-free! **800-929-2929** 7 am-9 pm Eastern Standard Time
Or fax your order to 802-864-7627
For fastest service order online: **www.bkconnection.com**

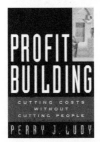

Profit Building
Cutting Costs Without Cutting People

Perry Ludy

Cultivating a loyal, productive workforce is crucial to business success. In *Profit Building*, Perry Ludy—who has worked for top companies in every major field from manufacturing to retail—introduces a five-step process called the PBP (Profit Building Process), which offers specific techniques for improving profitability by stimulating creative thinking and motivating teams to work together more effectively.

Hardcover, 200 pages • ISBN 1-57675-108-2 • Item #51082-415 $27.95

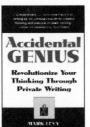

Accidental Genius
Revolutionize Your Thinking Through Private Writing

Mark Levy

Accidental Genius teaches readers how to better understand their world and create within it—using nothing more than pencil and paper or a word-processing program. Mark Levy has assembled an energizing and pragmatic body of writing techniques and shows readers how to use them as catalysts to achieve their own best thinking and business success. Readers will astonish themselves with the valuable insights they spray across their "private writing" pages—insights that can translate into thrilling projects, hefty money, and joy.

Paperback, 180 pages • ISBN 1-57675-083-3 • Item #50833-415 $16.95

How to Get Ideas

Jack Foster
Illustrated by Larry Corby

In *How to Get Ideas,* Jack Foster draws on three decades of experience as an advertising writer and creative director to take the mystery and anxiety out of getting ideas. Describing eight ways to condition your mind to produce ideas and five subsequent steps for creating and implementing ideas on command, he makes it easy, fun, and understandable.

Paperback, 150 pages • ISBN 1-57675-006-X • Item #5006X-415 $14.95

Berrett-Koehler Publishers
PO Box 565, Williston, VT 05495-9900
Call toll-free! **800-929-2929** 7 am-9 pm Eastern Standard Time
Or fax your order to 802-864-7627
For fastest service order online: **www.bkconnection.com**

Berrett-Koehler books and audios are available at quantity discounts for orders of 10 or more copies.

Driving Growth Through Innovation
How Leading Firms Are Transforming Their Futures

Robert B. Tucker

Hardcover, 240 pages
ISBN 1-57675-187-2
Item #51872-415 $27.95

To find out about discounts on orders of 10 or more copies for individuals, corporations, institutions, and organizations, please call us toll-free at (800) 929-2929.

To find out about our discount programs for resellers, please contact our Special Sales department at (415) 288-0260; Fax: (415) 362-2512. Or email us at bkpub@bkpub.com.

Berrett-Koehler Publishers
PO Box 565, Williston, VT 05495-9900
Call toll-free! **800-929-2929** 7 am-9 pm Eastern Standard Time
Or fax your order to 802-864-7627
For fastest service order online: **www.bkconnection.com**